Please Don't Take My Sisters

D0317162

Also by Maggie Hartley

LANCASHIRE COUNTY LIBRARY	
3011813887674 7	
Askews & Holts	13-Aug-2019
362.733092 HAR	£7.99
CPP	

Please Don't Take My Sisters

THE HEARTBREAKING TRUE STORY OF A YOUNG BOY
TERRIFIED OF LOSING THE ONLY FAMILY HE HAS LEFT

MAGGIE HARTLEY

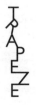

First published in 2019 by Trapeze,
an imprint of The Orion Publishing Group Ltd
Carmelite House, 50 Victoria Embankment,
London EC4Y 0DZ

An Hachette UK company

1 3 5 7 9 10 8 6 4 2

Copyright © Maggie Hartley 2019

The moral right of Maggie Hartley to be identified as
the author of this work has been asserted in accordance with
the Copyright, Designs and Patents Act of 1988.

All rights reserved. No part of this publication may be
reproduced, stored in a retrieval system, or transmitted
in any form or by any means, electronic, mechanical,
photocopying, recording, or otherwise, without the
prior permission of both the copyright owner and the
above publisher of this book.

A CIP catalogue record for this book is
available from the British Library.

ISBN (Paperback): 978 1 409 18899 5
ISBN (eBook): 978 1 409 18900 8

Typeset by Born Group
Printed and bound in Great Britain by Clays Ltd, Elcograf S.p.A.

MIX
Paper from
responsible sources
FSC
www.fsc.org FSC® C104740

www.orionbooks.co.uk

Dedication

This book is dedicated to Leo, Amelie, Lexie and Louisa, and all the children and teenagers who have passed through my home. It's been a privilege to have cared for you and to be able to share your stories. And to the children who live with me now. Thank you for your determination, strength and joy and for sharing your lives with me.

Contents

A Message from Maggie

I wanted to write this book to give people an honest account of what it's like to be a foster carer. To talk about some of the challenges that I face on a day-to-day basis and some of the children that I've helped.

My main concern throughout all this is to protect the children who have been in my care. For this reason, all names and identifying details have been changed, including my own, and no locations have been included. But I can assure you that all my stories are based on real-life cases told from my own experiences.

Being a foster carer is a privilege and I couldn't imagine doing anything else. My house is never quiet but I wouldn't have it any other way. I hope perhaps my stories will inspire other people to consider fostering, as new carers are always desperately needed.

Maggie Hartley

ONE

Back to Reality

Stepping off the plane, I breathed a sigh of relief as the cold air hit my face. I hated flying and I never truly relaxed until my feet were back on solid ground.

'Glad to be home?' asked my boyfriend Graham, squeezing my hand.

'Not really.' I smiled.

We'd just spent a blissful week in Turkey – it had been years since I'd had a holiday where I'd totally switched off. I hadn't been abroad for a long time, but Graham had found a bargain last-minute break and it was exactly what I needed to recharge my batteries. I was currently in between placements, something that very rarely happened. My last foster child, eight-year-old Tom, had gone back to live with his father, and with no new children on the horizon or any booked in for respite care, I'd decided to take advantage of this quiet patch.

The week had gone so quickly and now on this chilly spring day, we were back on British soil. As we queued up at passport control, I pulled my cardigan around my shoulders.

'Brrr, it's a bit nippier here than in Turkey.' I shivered.

We got through Immigration quickly and as we waited for our cases at the baggage reclaim, I finally turned my phone back on. As soon as it flickered into life, it began to beep and vibrate in my hand. I looked at the screen and my heart sank.

'Seven missed calls,' I gasped. They were all from the same number. It was my supervising social worker Becky from the fostering agency that I worked for.

'Welcome back to reality.' Graham smiled sympathetically.

'It's Becky,' I told him. 'I'd better ring her back as it must be important.'

'Of course.' He nodded. 'I'll get the cases.'

'Thanks, lovey,' I replied.

I'd been dating Graham, a physiotherapist in his forties, for years. I'd made it clear when I first met him that my fostering work always came first. He knew that, unlike a normal job, it was 24/7. On the whole he was very understanding, although I could tell he got fed up sometimes when I had a new child in or had a particularly challenging placement that meant I couldn't see him for weeks on end. But generally our low-key relationship suited both of us; we enjoyed each other's company and it was nice to meet up and go out for lunch or for a walk when we could.

I went over to a quiet corner and dialled Becky's number.

'At last!' she exclaimed. 'I've been trying to get hold of you all morning. Are you OK, Maggie?'

'I'm so sorry,' I told her apologetically. 'I've only just got off the plane.'

'Ah, I must have got my dates mixed up,' she sighed. 'I thought you were due back yesterday.'

2

'Well, we were supposed to be,' I replied.

I explained how our original flight had been grounded due to a mechanical fault. We'd had to spend the night at a hotel near the airport as there wasn't another flight until today.

'Is everything OK?' I asked her.

'I was ringing to talk to you about an emergency placement,' said Becky. 'But don't worry, I didn't realise that you'd just got back.'

'It's fine,' I reassured her. 'You didn't know that we'd been delayed. What is it?'

Becky explained that Social Services had three children that urgently needed a foster carer.

'All I know is that there are two girls and a boy and they've come into the care system very suddenly,' she told me. 'Sorry to be so vague but you know how it is, Maggie. Their social worker Alex is at court now waiting for them to issue an EPO.'

An EPO is an Emergency Protection Order and it was used by Social Services to take a child into care who they felt was at immediate risk.

'Don't worry, I'll try someone else,' she added. 'It doesn't feel fair asking you to take them if you haven't even got home yet.'

'Honestly, it doesn't matter,' I told her. 'Graham's just collecting the cases, so all being well, I should be back within the hour. I'd be happy to take them.'

I couldn't turn my back on three children in need just because I hadn't done my unpacking. Plus, I knew it was always hard to find someone with enough space to take on a larger sibling group. I hated the idea of them having to be split up and sent to different foster carers on top of the trauma of being taken into care.

When a new placement was arriving, I liked to be as organised and prepared as possible, but in reality it usually didn't happen that way. A lot of children were taken into care suddenly, and they turned up on my doorstep scared and bewildered, often having nothing with them apart from the clothes they were standing in. I'd been fostering for so long that I'd built up a stash of clothes and shoes for all ages and I had a huge cupboard of toiletries so I could generally cobble things together until I had chance to get to the shops. I had two spare rooms that I used for fostering and I always made sure that there was clean linen on the beds precisely for situations like this.

'Are you sure you're willing to take them?' asked Becky again.

'I'm absolutely positive,' I told her.

'Thanks, Maggie,' she sighed, sounding relieved. 'I know Social Services will be very grateful.'

'Please give the social worker my address and tell her that I should be there in an hour,' I added. 'Oh, and do you know how old the kids are?'

'I'm afraid I don't,' replied Becky. 'I don't know names or ages, just that there's three of them and that all this has happened today.'

'Not to worry, I guess I'll soon find out,' I said.

After Becky had put the phone down, I wandered over to where Graham was waiting with our suitcases.

'Everything OK?' he asked.

'You were right about getting back to reality.' I grinned. 'I've got a new placement on the way. Three children who've just been taken into care.'

'Already?' he gasped, raising his eyebrows in surprise. 'Wow, we'd better get you home ASAP then.'

On the drive back, my mind whirred with countless questions. What had happened to these children? What had they been through? Where had they come from? What sort of state were they in? Without knowing their ages, I didn't have a clue what to expect. They could be toddlers or teens or anything in between.

We were a few miles from my house when suddenly the traffic ground to a halt.

'Come on,' I muttered, looking nervously at my watch as we crawled along.

At this rate, it was going to take us well over an hour to get back. I hated the idea of the social worker arriving with three potentially distressed, frightened children and me not being there. I knew EPOs could be rushed through the courts very quickly – there was always a judge on standby to issue them if needed.

'What area are these kids coming from?' Graham asked, obviously sensing my panic.

'I don't know,' I told him. 'Hopefully it will take them a little while longer to sort out all the legal stuff.'

Thankfully the traffic eventually started moving again and twenty minutes later than planned, Graham turned into my road. My heart was thumping as we got closer to my house, but when we pulled up outside, I was relieved to see there was no one waiting on the doorstep.

'I'd invite you in, but I don't know how long I've got before these children turn up,' I told him.

'Don't worry, Maggie, I understand.' He smiled. 'You go in and get yourself sorted.'

It felt like such an abrupt end to what had been a wonderful break.

'Thanks for a lovely holiday,' I told him, giving him a quick kiss. 'I'll ring you when I can.'

I grabbed my case from the boot and walked up the front path. As I waved him off, I still felt really guilty, but I knew I needed to put that aside and focus on preparing as much as possible before the children arrived.

I turned my key in the lock and wheeled my case into the hallway. While I'd been away, my friend Carol had been round to check the house for me and she'd piled all the post on the hallway table.

I went into the living room and as I pulled open the curtains on the front window, I saw a car pull up outside, swiftly followed by another one behind it.

Blimey, they were here already.

I didn't have time to question why there were two cars. I had only a few seconds to put down my handbag and take off my cardigan before there was a knock at the door. I took a deep breath and opened it. A short, grey-haired lady in her fifties stood on the doorstep. She was wearing a creased black trouser suit and shirt, and she looked tired and harassed.

'Hi, I'm Alex the social worker,' she said, showing me her ID on the lanyard around her neck. 'You must be Maggie.'

'Nice to meet you,' I replied.

'Where are the children?' I asked, puzzled.

'I've left them in the car while we had a quick chat,' she explained. 'I've got two of them with me. The other one was driven here by her teacher. Poor Amelie hasn't been very well so Miss Hughes kindly offered to help me bring her over to you.'

'OK,' I said. 'Tell her to bring her in and she can lie down on the sofa.'

'We'll get Amelie in first, then I'll go and get the other two,' added Alex. 'I'm afraid they're in a bit of a state.'

I didn't even have a chance to ask what the names of the other two children were or what she meant by a 'bit of a state' before she'd disappeared back down the path. She went over to the other car, opened up the passenger door and lifted a little blonde girl out of the car seat. She looked to be four or five and had long blonde hair in curly ringlets and was wearing a school uniform.

A young woman who I assumed was Miss Hughes got out of the driver's seat.

'Come on, sweetie,' she said, taking Amelie's hand and leading her towards the front door.

The poor little mite was as white as a sheet and looked very wobbly as she walked towards me, clutching a carrier bag.

I crouched down to speak to her and was struck by the overwhelming smell of vomit.

'Hello, Amelie,' I said gently. 'I'm Maggie. I heard you're not feeling very well.'

The little girl shook her head sadly.

'I'm afraid she was sick a couple of times in the car on the way here,' said Miss Hughes apologetically, gesturing to the carrier bag in the girl's hand.

'Do you feel sick again now?' I asked Amelie, but she shook her head.

'Come in and you can lie down,' I told her.

I led her and the teacher into the living room. Amelie instantly lay down on the sofa and curled up. I covered her with a blanket and took the carrier bag off her.

'I'll just go and put this in the bin and then get you a bowl just in case you feel sick again,' I told her gently.

She nodded.

'Miss, where's Lexie and Leo?' she asked suddenly, looking worried.

'Remember, they're in the social worker's car,' Miss Hughes told her. 'They're just coming now.'

The two of us walked out into the hallway together.

'I'm Maria Hughes by the way.' She smiled. 'I'm Amelie's teacher.'

'The poor little thing looks really pasty,' I told her.

'Yes, she's got a bit of a tummy bug,'

There was no time to ask any more questions as there was suddenly a commotion outside.

'No!' screamed the child's voice. 'Don't wanna go to the lady's house.'

I looked out of the front door to see a little girl sitting on the path, kicking and screaming. She had the same blonde ringlets as her sister but was a few years younger. Alex had hold of her hand and was trying to pull her along.

'Come on, Lexie,' she urged. 'Amelie's inside waiting for you.'

'N-o-o-o,' she screamed. 'Don't. Want. To.'

Behind them, a figure climbed out of the back seat of the car. Given the girls' ages, I'd been expecting another little one so I was surprised when I saw a sullen older boy in school uniform. He was elfin-faced with straight brown hair and was clutching a couple of grubby-looking rag dolls in his hand. He went over to his sister.

'Lex, get up,' he told her gently. 'Amelie's in there and she's not feeling very well. She'll be dead scared and wondering where we've gone. Let's go and see her.'

'But I don't wanna go to the lady's house,' she screeched.

'I don't neither, but we haven't got a choice,' the boy told her.

Begrudgingly, the little girl got up, took her brother's hand and stomped up the path.

'This is Lexie and her big brother Leo,' Alex told me.

'Hello, you two, I'm Maggie.' I smiled. 'Come on in. Your sister's in the front room having a lie-down. Do you want to go in and join her while I talk to Alex?'

They both scowled back at me, neither of them saying a word. I ushered them into the living room and reluctantly they sat down on the sofa next to their sister.

'Are you OK?' Leo asked Amelie quietly, looking worried.

'I still don't feel good,' she whimpered, looking like she might cry.

I felt so sorry for her. All you wanted when you were ill was to be in the comfort of your own home, but here she was in a strange house being looked after by strangers.

All three of them looked shell-shocked. While Alex and Miss Hughes went into the kitchen, I tried to settle the children so we could have a chance to talk.

'Would any of you like a drink and a biscuit?' I asked.

They all shook their heads.

'Can I put the TV on for you?'

Again they shook their heads.

Suddenly Amelie reached for the bowl and was violently sick into it.

'Yuck,' screamed Lexie.

'I told you I weren't feeling good,' sighed Amelie, her face practically green.

I sat her up and went and got her some tissues and a glass of water and I cleaned out her sick bowl.

'There you go, lovey,' I said gently. 'Hopefully that will be the last of it now. When Alex has gone I'll get you cleaned up and we'll get you into bed.'

'What, we really have to sleep here?' sighed Leo.

'For tonight, yes,' I told him.

'For how long?' he snapped.

'I'm afraid I don't know that,' I replied. 'But hopefully we'll know more tomorrow. I need to go and talk to your social worker now so here's the remote just in case you change your minds about the TV. If you need me, just shout for me, OK?'

Amelie was almost asleep, Lexie shrugged her shoulders and Leo scowled at me, his eyes as dark as the shadows underneath them. What on earth had happened to these children and why had they been taken into care? I had to talk to their social worker as soon as possible.

As I walked out of the front room, I saw my suitcase standing in the hallway where I'd left it. Lazy days spent relaxing in the Turkish sunshine suddenly seemed like a very long time ago.

TWO

A Safe Place

In the kitchen Alex and Miss Hughes were sitting at the table waiting for me.

'Would you like a cup of tea?' I asked them. 'I know I could do with one.'

'Yes please,' replied Alex gratefully.

'I'd love a coffee.' Miss Hughes smiled. 'It's been quite a day.'

'I can imagine,' I sighed. 'Poor Amelie's really sick. As soon as you've gone, I'll get her to bed. Hopefully she'll feel better if she can sleep it off.'

I boiled the kettle and made everyone a drink before I asked any more questions.

'So,' I said, sitting down at the kitchen table. 'What can you tell me?'

'Not an awful lot in all honesty.' Alex shrugged. 'The children weren't known to us until we got a call from the school this morning.'

'So Amelie must be four if she's in reception?' I asked.

'She's just turned five.' Miss Hughes told me.

'Lexie is three and Leo is thirteen,' added Alex.

'Thirteen?' I questioned. 'Gosh, he's small for a teenager. I had him down as eleven or twelve at a push.'

'Yes, I suppose he is quite short for his age,' said Alex.

'So they're all siblings?' I asked, keen to double-check everything that I'd been told.

'Yes.' Alex nodded. 'Well, half-siblings. According to Leo, the girls have a different father. But from what I can gather so far, I don't think either dad is on the scene.'

Then came the most important question.

'So how did they come to be taken into care?' I asked.

Alex turned to Miss Hughes to answer. She explained that Amelie had started throwing up at school earlier so they'd phoned her mother to come and fetch her.

'We tried her mobile a couple of times but got no answer so we left a message,' Miss Hughes told me. 'The next thing we knew, Leo had turned up to collect her.'

'Does he often do that?' I asked.

'Lately, yes.' Miss Hughes nodded. 'In the past couple of months, we've seen him more than Mum. He drops Amelie off some mornings and picks her up and we had a note from home saying that was OK.'

In my head I couldn't help but wonder what impact that would have had on his own schooling, as most secondary schools start earlier in the morning than primaries.

'But because Amelie was so poorly today it didn't feel right sending her home with someone who is effectively still a child himself,' she added.

I nodded. At thirteen he shouldn't have had the responsibility of caring for a sick little girl. Besides that, he should have been at school himself.

'The office staff told him that we needed a phone call from his mum confirming that was OK or preferably for her or another adult to come up to school and collect Amelie. Leo argued the toss, got very angry and then stormed off.'

'What happened then?' I asked.

'We kept calling Mum but heard nothing and the mobile number she'd given us for an emergency contact was just ringing dead. Poor Amelie was being violently sick by then.

'I spoke to the head and after three hours we decided that instead of going round to the house ourselves, we would call Social Services,' she continued. 'I was hoping it was just a misunderstanding and they would trace Mum and she could come and get Amelie.'

Alex picked up the conversation from that point.

'I was hoping that would be the case too,' she told me. 'I called at the house at lunchtime. I knocked for ages and there was no answer, but I was sure I could hear a child inside.

'Eventually I went round the back and looked through the window and saw Lexie and a surprised-looking Leo and begrudgingly he let me in.'

'Where was their mum?' I asked.

'Oh, Mum was there,' replied Alex. 'Unfortunately, she was completely out of it on the sofa. Passed out in her underwear with an empty bottle of cider by her side.'

My heart sank.

'I checked that she was breathing OK and I managed to wake her up,' Alex told me. 'But she was so drunk she could barely stand up and she was swearing and very slurry. It was obvious that she wasn't in any fit state to look after a three-year-old and a sick five-year-old.'

She described how Leo was very angry.

'He was adamant that he could look after his sisters but I tried to explain that I couldn't leave them in the house,' Alex continued. 'I asked him if there was anyone else, such as a family member or a friend, who could come round or whose house they could go to, but he said it was just them.'

'What did Mum say about you taking the children?' I asked.

'She was too out of it to understand what was happening.' Alex shrugged. 'I tried to explain, but I don't think she took any of it in.

'I've left a note with my name and number asking her to give me a call so hopefully when she sobers up she'll be in touch.'

I couldn't imagine how frightening it would be to wake up and realise that someone had taken your children into care.

I hoped in a way this was a one-off incident, a moment of madness from their mum. Leo and Amelie's school uniforms were a little bit grubby and crumpled, but none of them were dirty or smelly and from what I'd seen of them so far, they looked fairly clean and generally well cared for.

'So I'm afraid that's all we know for now,' sighed Alex. 'We wanted to get them safe and settled somewhere over-night so Amelie can rest and then we'll see what tomorrow brings.'

'Do you think she needs to be seen by a doctor?' I asked.

'I think it's just a tummy bug,' replied Miss Hughes. 'It's been going round the class and it's usually gone in a couple of days.'

There were still lots of unanswered questions.

'When I'm back at the office I'm going to make some calls to try and build up a picture of what life is like for these children,' said Alex. 'I need to ring Leo's school as obviously he wasn't there today.

'Also, worryingly, when I saw Mum, I noticed that she was covered in bruises. She was black and blue all down one side and she looked like she had a black eye.'

'Did the kids say anything about it?' I asked.

'They've been through a lot today. Amelie was throwing up and Leo was still very angry, so I don't want to bombard them with lots of questions for now,' explained Alex.

'You're right.' I nodded. 'I'll get them settled, then hopefully we can find out more tomorrow.'

Miss Hughes finished off her coffee and picked up her handbag from the table.

'I hope you don't mind, but I'm going to have to head back to school now,' she said apologetically. 'I need to catch up on what I've missed today and update the head.'

'Of course,' said Alex. 'Thank you so much for your help. You did the right thing calling us.'

'We didn't have much of an alternative, really.' She smiled sadly.

'I could do with going back to the office too,' Alex told me. 'Is that OK with you, Maggie?'

'Yes, of course,' I told them. 'You both get off.'

'You know where I am if you need me, so keep in touch,' said Alex. 'On the way back I'm going to call in on Mum again to see if she's any more compos mentis, so I'll let you know.'

'What about Leo and school?' I asked her. 'Does he need to go in tomorrow?'

'Leave it for now,' Alex told me. 'I don't know how easy it is for him to get to his secondary school from here, but we'll know more in the morning.'

The three of us walked to the living room. Amelie, bless her, was practically asleep. Someone had turned the TV on and Lexie was curled up on Leo's lap watching cartoons.

'Bye, Amelie,' Miss Hughes told her gently. 'I won't see you tomorrow because you've been so sick but I hope you feel better soon.'

Amelie managed a weak smile.

'Bye, children,' said Alex. 'Maggie's going to look after you now and I'll be in touch tomorrow.'

'We don't need looking after,' snapped Leo.

'Well poor Amelie certainly does,' Alex told him. 'Try and get a good night's sleep.'

'What about our mum?' asked Leo, looking worried.

'I'm going to pop in and check on your mum on the way back to the office, so don't worry,' she reassured him.

By the time I'd closed the front door to them, I felt utterly exhausted. It was only late afternoon but after a four-hour flight and not a great night's sleep in the airport hotel the night before, I was shattered. I could have done with a bath and an early night, but I knew I needed to summon up all the energy I had to try and get these children settled. My first priority was to get Amelie cleaned up and put to bed.

'Come on then,' I told them. 'Let's all go upstairs and I'll show you where you'll be sleeping tonight.'

I noticed Leo was still clutching the two tatty rag dolls.

'What have you got there, sweetie?' I asked him.

'They're my sisters' favourites,' he told me. 'I made sure I brought them because I knew they wouldn't be able to sleep without them.'

'That was kind of you.' I smiled. 'You're obviously a very caring brother.'

'This is my one,' said Lexie, grabbing one of the dolls from Leo. 'She's called Flossie. And Amelie's one is Betsy.'

'Well let's take Betsy and Flossie upstairs and put them in your bedroom,' I told her.

Amelie was still very weak so I had to carry her up the stairs. I was determined give her a quick bath as she smelt of vomit and I could see that she had bits of it in her hair. I also wanted to give her a bit of time to get to know me rather than just putting her straight into a strange bed and leaving her to fall asleep.

'You'll be sleeping in here, girls,' I told them as I took them into the bigger bedroom.

There were bunk beds in here as well as a single bed which I gently put Amelie down on.

'Can I see sleep in the bunk bed?' asked Lexie excitedly.

'Of course, lovey.' I smiled. 'I think you'd be better on the bottom bunk if that's OK.'

While Amelie curled up on the bed and Lexie explored the room, I showed Leo the smaller single bedroom next door.

'You can sleep here,' I told him.

'Can't I sleep with the girls?' he asked.

'I do separate rooms at my house for bigger boys and girls,' I told him. 'Did you all sleep in the same room at home?'

He nodded.

'We only have two bedrooms.'

'Well I'm very lucky here because I've got two extra bedrooms, but don't worry, you're right next door to your sisters' room so you'll be able to hear them if they need anything.'

'All right.' He shrugged, although he didn't look too happy about it.

I left him in his room while I went to run Amelie a bath.

'Lexie, do you want to help?' I asked and she nodded.

I could see that she was curious to see the bathroom and I thought it would help make Amelie feel more comfortable and at ease if her sister was around too. She hardly said a word as I undressed her and gently lifted her into the bath.

'I'll be as quick as I can,' I soothed. 'Then we'll get you into some nice clean pyjamas and you can have a proper lie-down.'

I could tell that she was very weak and just wanted to sleep. When she was clean and dressed, she hobbled back to the bedroom. She willingly lay down and pulled the duvet up around herself.

'There's a glass of water on the bedside table,' I told her gently. 'If you feel sick, give me a shout and there's a bowl by your bed just in case, OK?'

But Amelie didn't say a word and I could see her eyes were already closing.

I took the other two back downstairs.

'Are you hungry?' I asked them and Lexie nodded.

But I knew I had a bit of a problem. What with being away on holiday for the past week, my fridge was virtually empty. I rummaged through the cupboards and found some tins of beans and tomato soup that would do, but I didn't have any of the basics.

18

I rang my friend Carol who lived around the corner. She was a foster carer too and I knew she had to pass my house on the way back from picking her foster children up from the local school.

'Please could you do me a massive favour?' I begged, when she answered. 'I've had three children come in suddenly and I desperately need a few bits from the shop. One of them is sick in bed so I can't go out.'

'Three kids?' she asked, sounding puzzled. 'Maggie, haven't you just got back from holiday?'

'I have,' I told her. 'I've only been home an hour and I haven't even unpacked yet, but Becky needed my help so I said I'd take them.'

'Oh, Maggie,' she sighed. 'What are you like? Just let me know what you need and I'll drop it in to you.'

'Thank you,' I said gratefully, reeling off a list.

I went back into the living room.

'My friend's going to drop me some bread off in a little while so how about beans on toast for tea?'

Leo shook his head. 'Lexie doesn't like beans,' he said firmly.

'They're yuck.' She grimaced.

Thankfully they both said they liked tomato soup. I put the telly back on and went to get them a drink of water. As I walked into the kitchen, I heard my phone beeping from the worktop. It was a text from Alex.

Called at Mum's. Knocked and knocked but no answer. Curtains drawn so couldn't see in but pushed another note through the door. Speak tomorrow.

I wondered what on earth had been going on in her life that had made her want to get blind drunk in the middle of the day? It was sad how many families I'd come across that had been destroyed by alcohol.

When I went back into the living room, Lexie was playing with a wooden doll's house that I had in the corner. Leo was just sitting there, deep in thought.

'Are you OK?' I asked him.

'I don't see why we've got to stay here,' he scowled. 'We'd have been fine at home. I could have managed.'

'I'm sure you'd have managed brilliantly,' I told him. 'But you're still a child and you shouldn't have to manage and Social Services have decided that you need to be somewhere safe with a responsible adult.'

'It's so unfair,' he snapped.

'I know you don't like being here and that's OK, but can you think of anything that you might like to do while you're here tonight?'

He shrugged his shoulders.

'Would you like to play a game?' I asked him. 'I've got Uno or Dobble. But I have to warn you, I'm very hard to beat at both of those.'

He shook his head. 'Never heard of them,' he sighed.

'What's your favourite TV programme then?'

'We didn't have any telly at home cos there was a row a few months ago and it got broke,' he replied.

'Well the TV's not broken here, so what would you like to watch?' I asked him.

'*Dr Who*?' he suggested.

'I'm sure I can find that for you.' I smiled.

While he was engrossed in *Dr Who*, Carol called and dropped the shopping off.

'I won't come in because I know you must be busy, but I hope it's going OK,' she told me, as she handed me a couple of carrier bags.

'Thanks.' I smiled. 'First nights are always tough, but they're doing OK. I'll give you a bell tomorrow,' I told her.

I got on with making the children tomato soup and cheese on toast. Leo just picked at his, but Lexie wolfed it down. We'd just finished eating when we heard shouting coming from upstairs.

'Leo?' a worried voice yelled. 'Leo?'

'That's Amelie,' he gasped, a concerned look on his face.

'I'll go and check on her,' I told him.

I bolted up the stairs. Amelie was wide awake, sitting up in bed. She was dripping in sweat and looked confused and terrified.

'Did you wake up and wonder where you were?' I asked her and she nodded, her lip wobbling.

'I want Leo,' she mumbled. 'Where's Leo?'

I carried her downstairs. As soon as she saw Leo, she clambered onto his lap and clung to him.

'Are we sleeping here?' she asked me with a scared look on her face.

'You're all staying here tonight while your mummy's not able to look after you,' I told her.

'But Leo looks after us,' she said matter-of-factly.

It was becoming increasingly apparent that Leo had been doing an awful lot for his sisters.

'I'm sure he does and I bet he's a brilliant brother, but sometimes even Leo needs looking after,' I tried to reassure her.

But rather than looking consoled, Amelie looked close to tears.

'I wanna go home, Leo,' she whispered to him, sounding scared. 'I don't wanna stay with the lady.'

'Me neither,' sighed Lexie, who looked like she was going to cry too.

'We can't,' Leo told her. 'They won't let us. We have to stay here but it will be OK. Then maybe we can go home tomorrow.'

I wanted to reassure them but I also didn't want to lie to them. I honestly didn't know what was going to happen over the next few days, as it all depended on what happened between their mother and Social Services.

'Let's get through tonight,' I told them gently. 'And then we'll see what tomorrow brings.'

To be honest, at that moment, I had no idea what that might be.

THREE

Being Mum

I'd done it. All three children were in bed at last and I was dead on my feet. Thankfully Amelie seemed to be feeling better – she'd even managed to eat a slice of toast before she'd gone back to bed. Then I'd given Lexie a bath and Leo had had a shower.

The girls were exhausted and to my relief, they'd quickly fallen asleep, both of them clutching their beloved rag dolls. Amelie was tired from throwing up all day and with Leo's reassurance, Lexie had calmed down and accepted the fact that they were staying here for the night, at least.

When it got to 9.30 p.m., I knocked on Leo's door to tell him it was time for him to go to sleep. I'd left a pile of books in his room ranging from basic chapter books to more complicated ones. Even though he was thirteen, I knew from past experience that I shouldn't assume that he could read. I'd fostered teenagers in the past who couldn't read the most basic picture books because they had missed so much school or had undiagnosed learning difficulties. But when I walked

23

into his room, Leo was engrossed in a Harry Potter book so it seemed that his reading was good.

'Time to turn your light out now, flower,' I told him gently.

'OK,' he sighed, putting the book down.

As he settled down in bed, he turned to me.

'Are we going back home tomorrow?' he asked, suddenly looking very young. 'Why won't you tell us?'

'Because I honestly don't know, lovey,' I told him. 'I wish I could tell you more, but I'm afraid I just don't know. Alex will come round to see you tomorrow and hopefully she'll have spoken to your mum by then and we'll know more.'

'But what if she can't talk to her?' he replied, worry etched on his face.

'The social worker will try really hard,' I told him. 'She needs to do that before anything can be decided.'

Leo looked so anxious.

'Try and get some sleep,' I urged him. 'You've had a hard day and you must be exhausted. My bedroom is just down the landing so if you want me, come and knock on my door and I'll wake up.'

'Why can't I sleep with my sisters?' he asked again.

'You're much older than the girls, so I think its best that you have your own bedroom,' I told him. 'You can stay up later and read, but you wouldn't be able to do that if you all shared a room.

'They're asleep now but their room is right next to yours and I've left their door open so you'll be able to hear them.'

There were no official rules from the local authority on siblings of different genders sharing bedrooms, but I tended to think that any older than ten and children were better off

24

having separate rooms. On a practical level, it made it easier to settle them to sleep and it meant they couldn't mess about or wake each other up.

'Get some sleep, lovey, and we'll hopefully know more tomorrow,' I told him.

Leo gave me a weak smile and turned over in his bed. It was so hard trying to reassure children when you were practically a stranger to them, with no real idea of what was going to happen yourself.

I went downstairs and flopped down on the sofa for what felt like the first time that day. I was just about to switch on the TV to unwind before bed when my phone rang. It was Louisa.

Louisa had come to live with me when she was thirteen after her parents were tragically killed in a car crash. She was twenty-three now and had lived with me up right up until a few weeks ago. She'd got married, and she and her husband Charlie had finally bought their own place. I missed her terribly and we'd swapped texts while I was away in Turkey.

'Maggie! Welcome home! How was the holiday?' she asked excitedly when I picked up. 'Are you feeling nice and chilled?'

'Erm, not really,' I replied, sighing.

I explained about the phone call from Becky.

'What?' she gasped. 'Are the kids there now?'

'They certainly are,' I replied. 'In fact, I've just got them all down for the night.'

'You must be shattered, Maggie,' she said.

'I am,' I sighed.

We chatted for a little while longer and Louisa said she'd pop round in the next few days for dinner.

'I can meet the kids.' She smiled.

'That's if they're still here,' I replied. 'It's all up in the air at the moment and I've got no idea how long they're going to be with me.'

I was desperate to go to bed but I knew I had to force myself to stay up a little while longer. Both girls were fast asleep, but I was concerned about Leo. I could already tell that he was a deep thinker and it was clear from Amelie and Lexie's behaviour that he had shouldered a lot of the responsibility of looking after his sisters. I kept thinking about him lying up there, listening to the unfamiliar sounds of a strange house; sounds that seemed extra loud when you weren't used to them, like the clicks my radiators made when the heating came on, or the chug of the boiler in the airing cupboard outside his bedroom. I wanted to make sure that he was settled before I turned in for the night.

I lasted until 10.30 p.m. when I knew I couldn't fight sleep any longer. I padded upstairs and clicked the stair gate on at the top. These children weren't toddlers but I did it just in case they woke up in the night and got disorientated. I didn't want to risk any of them falling down the stairs. I passed the girls' bedroom first and looked in on them. Much to my surprise, I could see a figure curled up on the floor between the bunk beds and the single bed.

Leo.

I gently woke him up.

'Come on, lovey, let's get you back to your own room,' I whispered, guiding him out onto the landing and into his bed.

He followed me groggily, and I was relieved when he fell straight back to sleep.

I knew that he wanted to sleep with his sisters, but I didn't want to encourage it in case they were with me for longer than one night.

Even though the children were settled, by the time I finally climbed into bed, I found that I couldn't get to sleep. My body was exhausted, but my mind was whirring as I wondered what tomorrow would bring and how long the children might be with me. I finally got to sleep around 3 a.m. but I was awake again by six, anxious in case the kids were already up. But as I crept to the bathroom, I couldn't hear any noise.

It wasn't until I came out of the shower that I could hear the girls stirring. I pulled on my dressing gown and on the way back to my bedroom, I popped my head around their door.

'Morning.' I smiled. 'Are you feeling any better, Amelie?'

She nodded back at me, looking sleepy, and I was relieved to see that she had a bit more colour in her cheeks than she had the night before.

'I'm just going to get dressed, then I'll take you both downstairs for breakfast. Can you remember where the bathroom is if you need the toilet?'

Both girls nodded sleepily.

I went into their room and lifted a box down from the top of the wardrobe.

'Here's some toys for you to have a look at while I get sorted,' I told them.

I crept past Leo's room and as I glanced through the crack in the door, I could see that he was still asleep.

I quickly got dressed and then went to get the girls. As we were about to head downstairs, Leo suddenly appeared on the landing. He looked bleary-eyed.

'Where are you taking them?' he asked accusingly.

'We're just going downstairs to have breakfast,' I told him cheerfully.

'I can give them breakfast,' he snapped. 'I know what they like.'

'It's fine,' I soothed. 'You give yourself chance to wake up. There's a dressing gown in there to put on so just come down and join us when you're ready.'

Amelie pushed her way past him and ran into his bedroom.

'Eurgh, it smells of wee wee in here,' she groaned, running back out holding her nose.

'No it doesn't,' snapped Leo, his face flushing bright red.

I looked through the door and I could see that his sheets had been pulled off and were rolled up in a ball on the floor. The poor lad must have wet the bed. Leo looked mortified and I didn't want to make a big deal of it.

'You can get yourself a shower if you want, sweetie,' I told him quietly. 'Then bring your pyjamas and sheets down and I'll pop them in the washing machine.

'Come on, girls,' I called, beckoning to Lexie and Amelie. 'Let's leave your brother to it.'

'He wees his bed at home sometimes,' Amelie said, as we went down the stairs.

I didn't say anything in response. I'd fostered several boys in the past who still wet the bed at twelve, thirteen and even older. Occasionally it was down to laziness, but usually it was due to anxiety. I was sure that was the case with Leo.

I got the girls a glass of milk each and some cereal and toast.

Amelie was still a bit pale and weak, but she was able to manage a bowl of cereal. Ten minutes later Leo came down. His hair was wet and I could see he'd had a shower. He wouldn't make eye contact as he handed me his wet sheets.

I got him some cereal and put out a plate of toast.

'Are we going home today?' asked Amelie as she reached out for a slice.

'I don't know what's happening at the moment, lovey,' I replied. 'I know Alex your social worker's trying to talk to your mummy so we'll see if she can get hold of her.'

'Maybe she's asleep,' sighed Lexie. 'Mummy sleeps lots.'

I could see the panicked look on Leo's face.

'My mum sleeps in the day sometimes because she has bad nights,' he explained to me, stepping in quickly. 'She's normally all right by about five when I give the girls their tea.'

'Do you give the girls tea every night?' I asked him casually.

'No,' he snapped. 'Just sometimes.'

Suddenly it was as if he realised what he'd just said and he quickly clammed up, his cheeks flushed.

'Why can't Tyrone look after us?' asked Amelie.

It was the first time I'd heard that name mentioned.

'No, not Tyrone. He hurts Mummy and he's mean. We don't want him,' said Lexie, shaking her head vehemently.

'Lexie, shush,' Leo scolded her.

I made a mental note to make sure I mentioned this conversation to Alex later on.

'Who's Tyrone?' I asked, keeping my tone light.

'Mummy's boyfriend,' replied Amelie. 'Well, sometimes he is and sometimes he isn't.'

'They do lots of shouting,' sighed Lexie.

I was about to ask them more questions when my mobile rang.

I could see it was Alex so I walked out of the kitchen into the living room so we could talk privately.

29

'Hi, Maggie, how are you doing?' she asked. 'How are the children?'

I quickly updated her and told her that Amelie seemed a lot better.

'Have you managed to get hold of Mum yet?' I asked her.

'Not yet,' she sighed. 'I'm about to go round there and try again.'

She explained that their mother, who we now knew was called Jade, had made an irate call to Social Services' out of hours line just after 4 a.m. that morning.

'She was shouting and swearing and demanding to know where her kids were and threatening to call the police,' sighed Alex. 'She'd obviously sobered up a bit, seen my note and realised what had happened. She was making all sorts of threats to the duty social worker and demanding to know your address.'

It was at times like this I was glad that my address was always kept confidential.

'I'll call round to the flat and speak to her, then I'll come and see you and explain what's happening to the children,' she told me.

'OK,' I said. 'Good luck. We'll be here.'

I went back into the kitchen where the children were still obediently sitting quietly at the table.

'Have you finished your breakfast, girls?' I asked them and they nodded.

'And, Leo, have you had your cereal?'

'Yeah,' he replied.

'No, you haven't, Leo, you tipped it down the sink,' shouted Amelie.

'Don't be such a tell-tale, Amelie,' he snapped.

'Are you sure you've had enough to eat?' I asked him.

'Sure.' He nodded.

I got them all a drink of water and started tidying the breakfast things away.

'Was that our mummy ringing on the phone?' asked Amelie, sounding hopeful. 'Is she coming to get us now?'

'That was your social worker Alex, who you met yesterday,' I replied. 'She's going to go round now to try and get hold of your mummy, then she'll come round here and see you.'

I'd already explained to the children that they wouldn't be going to school today, so I took them upstairs and dug out some clothes for them all. Leo went into his room to get dressed while I helped the girls.

They'd just finished having a wash and brushing their teeth when there was a knock at the door.

'Blimey, that was quick,' I said as I opened it to see Alex standing there.

'Any joy?' I asked her quietly.

She shook her head.

Just then all three children came thundering down the stairs.

The girls ran to Alex straight away; Leo hung back.

'Did you see our mummy?' asked Amelie.

'Are we going home now?' added Lexie.

'I'm afraid not,' Alex told them. 'Mummy wasn't able to talk to me. She did ring my colleagues last night though, so she knows that you're safe. I promise you I'll keep trying to get hold of her.'

The girls looked disappointed, but Leo didn't say a word.

I wanted to speak to Alex alone.

'Why don't you three play a game while I have a chat to Alex?' I asked them. 'I've got a cupboard full of games, so I bet you can find one that's lots of fun.'

'Can we watch TV, Maggie? Please can we watch cartoons?' pleaded Lexie, jumping up and down.

'OK, just for ten minutes,' I told her.

There wasn't anything wrong with TV, but I didn't want to shove them in front of it at every given opportunity. I needed something to keep them focused while Alex updated me, though, so I popped the telly on for them before Alex and I went into the kitchen.

'So Mum wasn't there?' I asked.

'She was, but sadly it was the same story as yesterday,' she replied. 'She was shouting and swearing at me through the letterbox, but she refused to answer the door.

'She was all over the place and it was obvious that she'd been drinking again.'

My heart sank. It was becoming clear that yesterday hadn't been a one-off occurrence.

'Was there a boyfriend there?' I asked her. 'The kids said their mum was seeing someone called Tyrone.'

'Not that I could see,' replied Alex. 'But I haven't managed to actually get into the flat yet, so who knows.'

'What happens now?' I asked.

'All I can do is keep trying until Jade is willing to talk to us, and until then the children stay with you,' she told me.

Alex also explained that she had spoken to Leo's secondary school.

'It's as we thought,' she sighed. 'He's missed a lot of school. At first it was just the odd day here and there, but according to his head of year, it's increased a lot over the past couple of months. Letters and emails have been sent home, but they've gone unanswered. They've tried to call Mum countless times but got no response.'

She explained how the school had contacted the local education authority, which had sent someone round to the flat but got no answer either.

'They were quite concerned about Leo and were about to call Social Services,' she added.

'I suspect from what Miss Hughes said about him doing the school run for Amelie that he's been covering for Mum quite a lot,' I sighed. 'Perhaps he's been staying off school to look after Lexie if Mum couldn't?'

'It's certainly looking that way,' said Alex.

Poor boy. He certainly had a heavy weight of responsibility on his young shoulders.

'Because we don't know how long Mum is going to be uncontactable, I think we need to get him back to school ASAP,' said Alex.

'If you could take him tomorrow, Maggie, that would be brilliant, just to ease him in,' she continued. 'In the meantime I'll work out his bus route from here and sort out a bus pass for him.'

'What about Amelie?' I asked.

'The same,' replied Alex. 'If she's better tomorrow, she should go in too. I think we should try and keep a little bit of normality for them.'

I wasn't sure that these children had had much in the way of normality in their lives recently, but I agreed with her that it was important to try and get them both back to school.

'What do you think about Lexie?' I asked.

Normally by three, children would be doing some nursery sessions, although there was no legal requirement.

'Jade hadn't enrolled her in the school nursery and as far as I'm aware, she isn't doing any nursery sessions at all,' Alex told me.

'With all this upheaval, it's not really fair to suddenly put her in nursery,' I replied. 'I'll take her to a few playgroups to ease her in gently and get her used to socialising with other children.'

'I think that's a great idea, Maggie, thanks.' Alex nodded.

When Alex had left, I told Amelie and Leo that I would be taking them back to school the following day. I was worried they were going to kick up a fuss, but they both seemed pleased.

'What about Lexie?' asked Leo, concerned. 'Where's she going to go?'

'Lexie's going to stay with me,' I told him.

'We'll find something really fun to do, won't we, Lexie?' I smiled.

'She likes watching telly,' said Amelie helpfully.

Just before lunch, Leo was in the kitchen with me while the girls were playing in the living room so I made the most of the opportunity to have a chat with him.

'Alex spoke to your teachers today and they said they've been really worried about you because you've been missing a lot of school lately,' I told him. 'How come you haven't been going in?'

He looked down at the floor and wouldn't make eye contact with me.

'I was helping my mum with the little ones cos she's not been well,' he said defensively.

'What sort of not well?' I coaxed him gently.

'Oh, she was just ill, and like I said before she's not very good in the mornings. She likes to sleep.'

'I wonder if you've had to take Amelie to school and look after Lexie because your mum's been drinking?' I said aloud.

I often found that suggesting things in this way rather than explicitly asking them was a good technique to use, as it was a bit gentler and less judgemental. It also alleviated some of the responsibility on a child to not betray their parent. Rather than ask Leo a direct question or accuse his mum of drinking, it was more about me pondering it out loud.

Anger flickered across Leo's face.

'No, she hasn't!' he yelled. 'You've got it wrong. She only drinks sometimes when she's had a bad time.'

'I'm sorry, Leo, I didn't mean to upset you,' I told him gently. 'Alex and I are just trying to find out what things are like at home for you and your sisters and work out how we can help you.'

'We don't need your help,' he spat. 'You don't know my mum, you don't know nothing. Why are you all poking your noses in? We can manage, we don't need anyone to help us. I don't see why we can't go home.

'Please just leave us alone,' he begged.

He got up off the sofa and stormed out of the living room, slamming the door behind him.

My heart felt heavy for Leo. I was desperate to help him and his sisters, but I knew I seemed like the enemy to the children, keeping them away from their home and their mum. Sadly, though, sometimes home wasn't the safest place to be.

FOUR

The Unknown

Driving into the supermarket car park, I spotted a space and pulled into it.

I was determined to make the most of Leo and Amelie not being at school today and use the afternoon to get organised. It felt like we were in limbo, as we had still been unable to establish contact with the children's mother, Jade. Alex had called round to the flat three times so far today but there had been no answer at any point, so we still had no idea how long the children were going to be with me. Alex had posted her card with the date and time on it each time, asking Jade to ring her urgently, but there had still been no word. It was unfathomable that her children had been taken into care and yet nearly 24 hours later she still hadn't bothered to get in touch to find out where they were and how they were getting on.

'Why have we come here?' scowled Leo as I grabbed a trolley.

He was still in a bad mood with me after he'd stormed off earlier when I'd asked him about his mum.

'Because I need to get you all some clothes and underwear,' I explained, leading them all straight to the clothing section.

Amelie and Lexie looked as though Christmas had come early when I told them they could each choose an outfit for themselves, as well as some pyjamas, and were having lots of fun looking at all the different options.

'What about some bobbles and clips too, to put in that lovely hair of yours?' I asked them once they'd each chosen.

The girls squealed with excitement and I could see that it was a novelty for them to come shopping. With their ringlet curls and big blue eyes, they looked like two little dolls skipping up and down the aisles. Leo shuffled awkwardly behind them, keeping a protective eye on his sisters as always.

Once I'd finished kitting the girls out, we walked over to the boys' department.

'I don't need anything,' snapped Leo, before I could say a word.

'We need to get you a few bits and pieces to tide you over, lovey,' I explained. 'I washed the uniform that you came in yesterday but you'll need some other clothes too,' I told him.

With school uniform, I worked on the principle of three sets per child: one to wear, one spare and one in the wash.

'Well, I'm not trying anything on,' he said defiantly.

I picked up a packet of three white school shirts and rummaged through a rail of grey trousers until I found an age thirteen pair.

'I told you I'm not trying anything on,' repeated Leo.

'I need to know that they fit you OK,' I told him.

'Nope,' he said firmly, shaking his head.

I could see that no matter what I said, there was no persuading him. I held the trousers up against him but they looked like they'd swamp him. He was small for his age and very slight. The clothes I'd managed to dig out of my cupboard for him were aged twelve, but I could see they were way too big for him. The top was baggy and hung off him and I could see all the extra material around the waist of the jeans. I settled on age ten trousers, which looked to be the closest fit and a nine to ten blazer.

'Do you need anything else for school?' I asked him.

'No,' he snapped.

'Are you sure there's nothing you could do with?' I replied.

'Well maybe a pencil case, some pens and a ruler and a compass.' He shrugged. 'Then I don't have to borrow my mate's. And a bag to put them all in. I normally have a JD Sports carrier bag but I've left it at home.'

'We can sort all of that.' I smiled.

Suddenly Leo stopped dead in his tracks.

'Why are you doing this?' he asked, looking suspicious. 'Why are you buying us all this stuff? Are we staying with you for good now and you're not telling us?'

'I know I sound like a broken record, flower, but the truth is we don't know what's going to happen until Alex can talk to your mum,' I told him. 'At the moment she can't get hold of her or get into your flat to get clothes for any of you, so I need to buy you some to tide you over.

'Whatever I buy today belongs to you and if you go back home then you can take them with you,' I continued. 'OK?'

Leo shrugged his shoulders grumpily but it seemed to appease him a bit, and the rest of the supermarket trip passed without incident.

The rest of the afternoon was spent quietly at home, and that night I made sausages and mash for tea. The girls tucked in eagerly, but Leo just picked at his food.

'Leo, please try and eat something,' I pleaded. 'You need to keep your strength up.'

'OK,' he said reluctantly, although it was clear that every mouthful was a struggle.

By the end of the meal, I was relieved to see that he'd eaten a sausage and most of his peas. But as I cleared the table and scraped the plates, I realised that both of the sausages as well as the peas were hidden under the pile of mash. He'd been moving the food around his plate but he'd hardly eaten anything. Poor lad. I could see he was anxious and was no doubt feeling nervous about going back to school tomorrow.

In the morning, Leo was awake first and without me asking him, he went and woke the girls up.

'Lex, Am, it's breakfast time and then you need to get ready,' he told them.

I could see from the way that he ushered them downstairs and the prompts that he gave them to brush their teeth and wash their face with a flannel that this was something that he was used to doing. He knew their morning routine and was adept at helping Amelie get ready for school and getting her out of the house on time. When we got in the car, he was insistent that we drop Amelie first.

'It will mean that you're late,' I told him, but I could see it was important for him to have the reassurance that Amelie was safely in school.

Her primary school was a twenty-minute drive away, and as we parked up and walked into the playground, Amelie suddenly looked unsure. She grabbed Leo's hand.

'It's going to be all right, Amelie,' he told her gently. 'You'll be fine. You can see your friend Lacey and I'll see you back at Maggie's tonight.'

'OK.' She smiled. 'Bye, Lexie,' she said to her little sister.

'Have a good day, flower,' I said. 'Look, Miss Hughes is over there waiting for you.'

The teacher walked over to us. 'How are you feeling, Amelie?' she asked her gently.

'Better.' She nodded. 'But we're still at Maggie's house. We haven't gone back to our mummy yet.'

'Oh dear, I'm sorry to hear that,' she replied, looking concerned. 'But I'm sure Maggie's been taking good care of you.'

We waved goodbye to Amelie as Miss Hughes led her into the classroom, and Leo seemed reassured. Then I drove him to his secondary school. I went in with him to explain to the receptionist why he was late and to give them my contact details in case there were any problems and they needed to get hold of me. Thankfully Leo seemed happy about going to school, so I didn't have to worry about him making a scene.

'Bye, Lexie,' he said, bending down and giving her a kiss on the cheek. 'Be a good girl and I'll see you tonight.'

She nodded and waved.

'Don't forget your packed lunch,' I yelled, handing it to him before he could disappear off down the corridor.

As Lexie and I drove back home, I was relieved both children had gone off to school without a fuss.

'Now, what shall you and I do?' I asked her when we walked in the door. 'How about some painting, or maybe we could do some stickers?'

Lexie shook her head.

'I wanna watch telly,' she said firmly.

I hesitated, but I knew I could do with a little bit of time to update my notes and email them to Alex.

'OK,' I agreed. 'But just for ten minutes.'

I settled beside her on my tablet and worked on my notes, as Lexie watched the television. I glanced over at her, her eyes glazed over and glued to the cartoons on the screen and I knew I was getting an insight into what her days at home had been like. I felt really sad for her. She was totally and utterly zoned out. All hell could have broken loose in front of her, but she wouldn't have noticed or moved.

I made sure to stick to the ten minutes that I'd promised her.

'Come on then, let's go and make a snack,' I told her when the time was up and the adverts came on from the programme she'd been watching.

'No, I wanna watch more telly,' she grumbled, shaking her head defiantly and still staring fixatedly at the screen.

I went over and turned it off. Lexie's mouth gaped open in shock, as though she couldn't believe what I had done.

'Remember I said it was just for ten minutes when you started watching,' I told her. 'You can watch it again later when Amelie and Leo get home from school.'

Lexie crossed her arms and stomped her feet, her lip starting to wobble, and I could tell she was about to throw the mother of all tantrums. But before that could happen, I did my best to distract her.

'Have you seen my amazing dollies?' I asked her, pointing to the toy box in the corner. 'They've got their own pram and even a high chair.'

Thankfully the promise of new toys did the trick. Whenever Lexie asked about putting the TV on, I pointed out something else that I thought she'd like. I could see it was going to take a while to wean her off the expectation of constant TV.

I also decided that whenever I did allow her a little bit of TV in the day, I would make sure that I was sitting with her so I could talk to her about what we were watching. That way, it would become more of a social thing, instead of me plonking her in front of a screen and using it as an electronic babysitter.

Later that afternoon, we went to pick up Leo and Amelie from school. They were both very quiet and seemed exhausted. I think the trauma of the past two days was catching up with them. We collected Leo first as he finished earlier. As we were driving back, I showed him the bus stop where he could get the bus to my house. I was happy to drop him off in the mornings but I knew that as a teenager, it would be good for him to have some independence and he was perfectly capable of getting himself back to my house.

They both said they'd had a good day at school so I got them a snack and unpacked their bags. When I took Leo's lunchbox out, I could see that it was untouched.

'How come you didn't eat your lunch, Leo?' I asked him. 'You must be starving.'

'Oh, my mate John bought me some chips from the canteen instead,' he replied casually.

'Would you prefer to get food at school instead of taking a packed lunch?' I asked him.

'All my mates do that.' He shrugged.

I agreed that from now on I'd send him with some money to buy his own lunch. What struck me as odd was that another whole day had passed and neither Amelie nor Lexie had asked about their mother. They'd even stopped asking about when they were going to go home, which was strange. What I did notice was they were very clingy around Leo. If he wasn't in the room, they wanted to know where he was, and it was clear that he was their security blanket.

The following morning, when Lexie and I got back from the school run, Alex called me.

'Any updates?' I asked her. 'Have you got hold of Mum yet?'

'I'm at the end of my tether with that woman,' Alex sighed. 'She's been giving me the runaround for two days now.'

She explained that she had gone to the flat again the day before.

'She still wouldn't open the door to me but for once, she was up and about and she didn't seem drunk,' she told me.

That sounded like progress.

'She said that she wanted to have a shower before we spoke, so she asked me to call back in an hour,' continued Alex. 'I explained that I wanted to help her see the children and talk through everything.'

'So what happened?' I asked, although I already knew the answer.

Alex explained that when she'd gone back, Jade didn't answer the door or the phone and there was no sign of her.

'So we're back to square one,' she sighed.

I could understand her frustration. It was Friday today so I knew nothing was going to change over the weekend.

'I'm going to give it one last try on Monday, then I'm going to speak to my manager,' she told me. 'Decisions have to be made about the children's future and if Mum won't engage, they'll have to be made without her.'

It was frustrating and sad, especially for Leo, Amelie and Lexie.

'OK, I'll explain to the kids what's going on,' I told her.

I waited until Friday evening when they'd got back from school.

'I spoke to Alex this morning and she got hold of Mummy, but she's not going to be able to speak to her until next week,' I told them. 'So that means you're definitely going to be with me this weekend. Shall we plan something fun for us all to do?'

'Yeah!' said the girls, excitedly, and began chattering away loudly to each other with ideas.

Leo didn't say a word and a few minutes later I noticed him going upstairs. I left him for ten minutes before I went to check on him. I tapped on his bedroom door and went in to find him lying on his bed, staring at the ceiling.

'So she doesn't want us back then,' he sighed. 'And you're just not telling us.'

'It's not that, lovey,' I replied. 'Alex genuinely can't speak to her until next week.'

'Well if she wanted us back, then she'd speak to her, wouldn't she?' he sighed.

He looked so sad, it was heartbreaking.

'Just let us go home, then I can make sure that she talks to you,' he said desperately. 'If I'm at home, then I can make sure it will be OK. I promise I'll go to school more and I can help my mum.'

His eyes filled with tears.

'You were right,' he sighed. 'She does drink. But not all the time and only if she's had a fight with Tyrone. But if I'm there I can try my best to make her not drink.'

I sat down next to him.

'Lovey, that's not your responsibility,' I told him gently. 'Your mum needs to be looking after you, not you looking after her. Besides, what will happen when you're at school or not there? What will happen to Lexie if your mum's been drinking?'

'Oh, she'll be OK.' He nodded. 'She's done it before. I put the telly on for her and leave her some lunch. And I can pick Amelie up from school.'

I couldn't imagine what life had been like for this poor lad, constantly worrying and wondering what sort of state his mum was going to be in each day.

As he was talking to me, I could see that he was chewing his lip. He was a bundle of anxiety and nerves.

'Leo, three-year-olds can't be left on their own. If your mum's passed out drunk, she's not actually looking after Lexie, and what if she does something silly?'

By now I noticed he'd bitten so much skin off his lip that it was bleeding.

'Oh, lovey, your lips are bleeding,' I told him gently.

I fetched a tissue for him.

'I've got a bad habit of chewing my lips,' he told me, not meeting my eyes.

'Maybe you do that when you're worried about something?' I suggested.

'I'm not worried,' he snapped. 'I just don't understand why Mum won't talk to the social worker so we can go home.'

'I know,' I sighed sympathetically. 'Hopefully she will next week.'

That night when the kids were in bed, I sat down at the computer and typed up my notes for the day. These were any bits of practical information about the children that I would send to Alex.

I made a record of the conversation that I'd had with Leo.

What's starting to become clear is that not only has he shouldered a lot of the responsibility for looking after his sisters, he's also been taking responsibility for his mum. He sees his role as somehow trying to keep her on the straight and narrow, I wrote. *He thinks that if they go home, then he can make it all right.*

I no longer found myself surprised by how loyal most children were to their birth parents. They could have suffered the most awful abuse and neglect at their hands and yet they knew no different, so even the neglect is familiar to them and they want nothing more than to go home. It was distressing to see this pattern showing itself in Leo.

On Saturday morning I did what I always did and tackled my washing pile. I noticed Leo's wet sheets were piled up by the laundry basket. He had wet the bed again, and although I felt desperately sorry for him, I wasn't surprised after everything that he'd been through in the last two days. I sorted out the school uniforms and as I picked up Leo's blazer, I heard something jangling in his pockets. I put my hand in and realised that it was the two-pound coins that I'd given him for his school lunch.

'Leo, you didn't spend your dinner money,' I told him. 'What did you have for lunch?'

He looked a bit sheepish.

'Oh, my mate Ryan had loads of sandwiches so he gave me some,' he muttered. 'His mum always gives him massive lunches and he can't eat them all.'

Typical teenager, I thought to myself. I'd fostered enough older boys to know that their idea of a good lunch was often a can of pop and a packet of crisps.

In the afternoon I was determined to do something fun with the children to help take their minds off things. It was pouring down and very gloomy for a day in early May so I decided to take them swimming.

'Yay!' grinned the girls when I told them.

'I've got some swimming stuff that will fit you all that you can borrow,' I told them.

'I'm not going,' sulked Leo. 'It's too cold.'

'My local pool is normally nice and warm,' I told him. 'And there's a waterslide too.'

'I said, I'm not coming,' he hissed.

Amelie looked close to tears.

'Please, Leo,' she begged. 'Please come with us. We haven't never been swimming before and we need you to help us.'

The longer the children were with me, the more I could see that the girls very much relied on Leo to feel secure, both of them always looking to him for reassurance.

'OK,' he sighed. 'I'll come but I'm not getting in the water.'

He seemed very insistent and I wondered if it was because he couldn't swim and was perhaps embarrassed about it.

Before we left, I did the girls' hair. I was trying to put Lexie's hair in a bobble but she was wriggling around and fussing.

'No, no, no,' she wailed. 'I don't like it. I want Leo to do it.'

He came rushing over.

'She doesn't like tight bobbles,' he told me. 'Amelie doesn't mind, but Lexie prefers a clip or a hair band.'

Once again, it struck me how much responsibility Leo took for his sisters and how much he cared for them. His relationship with them was so different to most teenage boys and their little sisters. It was clear that he knew exactly what they liked and disliked, even down to how they liked their hair done.

When we got to the leisure centre, Leo was still adamant that he wasn't coming in.

'Well if you want to come through to the pool with us, you'll have to get changed,' I told him.

The girls looked pleadingly at him.

'All right,' he sighed.

The girls insisted on going into a family cubicle with Leo so he could help them get changed. I went into one next to them.

When they came out, the girls were jumping up and down with excitement. Leo had got changed but he had his towel firmly clutched around him under his armpits. He still refused to go into the water so while I went into the baby pool with the girls, he sat on the edge, his towel still firmly wrapped around him.

Neither Lexie nor Amelie could swim, so I put armbands on them both and I could tell they were nervous, despite their initial excitement. In fact, Lexie insisted on staying close to Leo at all times, clinging onto the side where he sat. At one point, she reached out to him and as he leaned over to hold onto her arms, his towel fell down to his waist. It was only for a second before he frantically pulled it up again, looking panicked, but I was shocked by what I saw. I had always known that he was petite for his age, but seeing him in just his swimming trunks, I was horrified by how painfully thin he was. His chest was practically concave and his ribs clearly jutted out. Alarm bells began to ring about his eating habits, or, more accurately, the lack of them. I suddenly realised that he might not be telling me the truth about friends giving him lunches at school and I felt sick at the thought of him starving himself.

I didn't say anything to him and carried on playing with the girls, but my mind was whirring with worry. To my relief, the girls started to relax and enjoy splashing around in the water, but the shocking sight of Leo's frail, bony torso niggled at me for the rest of the weekend.

When Alex phoned me on Monday morning, I told her about my worries.

'At first I thought it was a case of him just being a fussy teenager, but he's barely eaten since he got here and he's so thin,' I explained.

'Well, he is very small-framed,' she told me. 'Perhaps there wasn't a lot of food around at home?'

'But the girls seem fine,' I said. 'They don't look underweight.'

'It sounds like something we just need to keep an eye on,' Alex told me, sounding unconcerned.

'You're probably right,' I sighed.

On Sunday, I cooked a roast chicken and invited Louisa and Charlie round to meet the children. Leo didn't say much and made himself scarce upstairs, and although the girls were very shy at first, they soon warmed to Louisa. She'd just had a manicure and they loved her red, glossy nails, so while I sorted out the lunch in the kitchen, she painted their nails for them with some glittery pink varnish that I had in my bathroom cabinet.

She came in later to give me a hand serving it all up.

'What sweet little girls,' she sighed. 'They're very cute.'

'They are.' I smiled. 'They're like two little dollies.'

From what I had seen of these children so far, it was clear that Leo had done his best to shield the girls from what was going on at home. He had stepped up to be their parent and their protector when their mum couldn't, and consequently they didn't seem to have as much anxiety as he had. It would explain why they hardly ever asked about their mum. Leo was the person who they relied on for love and security.

We all sat down together and I was pleased to see Leo tucking into his roast. In fact he couldn't wolf it down quickly enough.

'Wow, someone was hungry,' laughed Charlie as he saw his clean plate.

'Please can I have some more, Maggie?' he asked and I was more than happy to oblige.

As I watched him demolish his second plateful of food, I felt reassured. Alex was right; food had probably been scarce for him at home and, having seen how much he took care of his little sisters, I wouldn't have been surprised if he'd prioritised feeding them over his own hunger. I reasoned that it was probably going to take Leo a little while to put some weight on. It would turn out to be the least of my worries.

FIVE

Hidden Secrets

Within the first few days of a child being taken into care, they have what's known as a looked after child (LAC) medical. Foster carers or social workers take them to see a LAC consultant who works for the local authority and will measure their height, weight, take their blood pressure and discuss any health concerns. On Monday morning, Leo, Amelie and Lexie were due to have theirs. The girls seemed intrigued about it, but Leo wasn't happy.

'I don't see why we have to go,' he sighed in the car on the way there. 'There's nothing wrong with us.'

'It's just a standard thing that every child has to do,' I told him. 'You'll be in and out of there in ten minutes. I've known Trisha for years and she's very nice.'

But nothing would reassure him. I took the girls in first while he waited outside.

'Maggie, it's so lovely to see you.' Trisha smiled as we entered.

She'd been the LAC consultant for my local authority for years and I'd brought countless foster children to her.

Lexie and Amelie were as good as gold. They were fascinated by the blood pressure monitor and the scales and they obediently did everything Trisha asked them to.

'We've got two healthy girls here.' She smiled. 'Now where's your brother. Leo, isn't it?'

'He's outside,' I told her. 'I'll just go and get him.'

The girls and I walked out to the waiting room where we'd left Leo. He was curled up in a ball on the chair, his knees clutched tightly to his chest.

'Leo, we did it and we got a sticker,' Lexie told him proudly.

'It was fine, Leo,' Amelie said, tapping him on the arm. 'The lady's nice and it didn't hurt.'

'Are you OK, lovey?' I asked him. 'What's wrong?'

He started to rock backwards and forwards.

'I don't want to do it,' he whispered, his head buried in his knees.

I sat down in the chair next to him and put my hand on his shoulder to try and calm him down.

'Leo, flower, it's just a standard check-up that every child coming into the care system has to have,' I told him. 'Like the girls said, it's nothing scary, it will only take a few minutes and it's not going to hurt.'

'I said, I'm not doing it,' he hissed.

'I'll come in with you if you want,' I said gently. 'Trisha's very nice and she's waiting for you.'

He kept on rocking backwards and forwards in his chair.

'Noo,' he wailed. 'I'm not going in there.'

There were a couple of other people in the waiting room and they looked up as Leo's voice rose.

'Nobody's going to make you do anything you don't want to do,' I murmured gently. 'You don't have to take any of your clothes off if that's what's bothering you. Trisha can weigh and measure you with your clothes on if that makes a difference?'

'I don't care,' he hissed. 'I'm not doing it. You can't make me.'

He was right. I couldn't physically force him.

I went to see Trisha and explain what had happened.

'He's refusing point-blank to come in, I'm afraid,' I told her.

'I'll have a chat to him just in case that helps,' she replied sympathetically.

She came out into the waiting room and introduced herself to Leo. He refused to look at her, his face still buried in his knees.

'Leo, tell me what you're worried about?' she asked him kindly. 'What is it that you don't want to do?'

'I don't want anyone messing with me,' he said.

'All I'm going to do is measure your height and check your weight and blood pressure,' she told him patiently. 'You'll just need to stand on some scales and I'll also put a special machine around the top of your arm to check your blood pressure.'

'I don't care,' he yelled. 'I'm not doing it.'

It was obvious that he wasn't going to change his mind and there was nothing that we could do about it.

'OK, we'll leave it for today,' Trisha told him, raising her eyebrows at me. 'I just need to quickly talk to Maggie about a few things.'

She asked the woman working on the reception desk to keep an eye on the three of them – Amelie and Lexie were happily playing in the toy corner and seemed totally oblivious to what was going on.

I followed Trisha into her office.

'Have you got any immediate concerns about him?' she asked.

'My main worry is his weight,' I explained. 'He's very skinny and he's not eating much at all. Also, he's been wetting the bed most nights since he arrived, although I know that's probably related to the trauma that he's been through.'

I was hoping that, as he felt more settled at my house and his anxiety settled, the incidents of bed-wetting would stop.

'Well, unless he consents, I can't force him to get weighed,' she sighed.

'Let's make him another appointment in a couple of weeks if he's still in the system and hopefully then we can persuade him. If you've got any urgent worries in the meantime, go and see the GP,' she continued.

Leo couldn't get out of that place quick enough. As soon as we walked out into the car park, I saw him relax and my heart went out to him. I knew there were all sorts of reasons why the idea of having a medical might have unsettled him. We'd put him in yet another unfamiliar situation with unfamiliar people. Over the past few days, he'd had so much change and so much to cope with, it wasn't surprising that he was reacting against it. I could see he couldn't wait to get back to the safety and familiarity of his school.

Once I'd dropped him and Amelie off at their separate schools, Lexie and I headed home. We'd just walked in the door when Alex phoned.

'Good news,' she told me. 'I've just got hold of Jade and she's agreed to talk to me.'

'Finally,' I sighed. 'What a relief. When are you going round?'

'She said she'd prefer to come into the office and talk to me as her boyfriend was at the flat,' Alex explained. 'She also demanded that I had the children there so she could see them, but I told her I can't organise a contact session until I've talked to her and we know more about what's going on. She's coming in this afternoon so I'll let you know how it goes, then perhaps we can sort out a contact for tomorrow?' she asked.

'That's fine by me,' I said, just relieved that at last we might get some answers and be able to update the children.

Just as Lexie and I were getting ready to go and pick up Amelie from school, Alex called back.

'How did it go?' I asked her.

She described how Jade had turned up with a black eye and a fresh cut on her cheek.

'I asked her how it had happened, and she said Tyrone didn't like her talking to me,' sighed Alex.

Sadly, I wasn't surprised. Some of the things the children had said had already raised my suspicions that Jade was in a violent relationship.

'She's absolutely outraged that the children have been taken into care,' said Alex. 'She was ranting and raving that the school was so fussy and Leo could have just collected Amelie.'

'Did you ask her about the drinking?' I asked.

'I did and she said it wasn't illegal and what was the problem with it?

'I told her how concerned we were about the children,' continued Alex. 'That her daughter was ill at school and no one could rouse her to go and collect her. Her view was that it wasn't a problem, as Leo could do it. She said she was asleep because she'd had a bad headache.'

Alex also explained that Jade was under the impression that she could have the children back.

'She seemed to think that as soon as she'd spoken to me it would all be sorted out and they could come home, so I had to explain that it wasn't as simple as that. I said I'd been trying to get hold of her for a week. She said she'd been busy and hadn't been feeling well.'

It was gobsmacking to hear how little interest she seemed to have in her own children and their welfare.

'So, what happens now?' I asked.

'We agreed that she can see the kids as soon as possible, so I'm going to set up a contact session tomorrow after school,' she told me. 'In the meantime, I'm also going to organise a professionals meeting for next week.'

A professionals meeting was where me, Alex, the children's teachers and everyone involved in their day-to-day care would get together and discuss the children and any concerns that we had and decide what the best plan was going forward.

'I was very clear with Jade that the kids won't be going back to live with her until we have made some decisions at the meeting.'

'What did she make of that?' I asked.

'She was outraged. Couldn't see why her kids had been taken off her. Saw nothing wrong with her behaviour whatsoever.'

I knew how hard it could be for parents to accept when their children were taken into care by Social Services, but Jade really did seem to be in denial about what was happening.

At least I had something to tell the children at last, though. When they got home from school that night, I chatted to them as we ate dinner.

'Alex rang me today,' I told them, as I dished out the fish fingers. 'She talked to your mummy and she'd really like to see you, so we thought we'd sort it out for tomorrow after school.'

The girls smiled.

'Is Mummy coming here?' asked Amelie, her blue eyes lighting up with excitement.

'How will she find us?' asked Lexie. 'She doesn't know where your house is.'

I could see Leo was deep in thought.

'So shall we go and pack up our stuff then?' he asked.

Bless him, the poor lad thought that I meant they were going home.

'No, flower,' I explained gently. 'You're still going to be staying here for the time being, but tomorrow you can go and see your mum for an hour. You'll go and see her at a building called a contact centre.'

I explained to them what a contact centre was and how I would drop them off and there would be a room with toys, books and a sofa and a little kitchen where they could get a drink.

'Why can't we just go home and see her?' Leo scowled. 'They've spoken to her, now what more do they want?'

'Social Services needs to be sure that your mum can look after you all properly,' I explained gently. 'Alex has organised a meeting next week so we'll know more then, but in the meantime you can still see your mum.'

The following afternoon it was time for contact. Amelie and Lexie seemed excited but Leo was, as always, a lot quieter than his little sisters. As we walked across the car park to the contact centre, the girls skipped along happily.

'Are you OK? I asked Leo. 'Are you looking forward to seeing your mum?'

'Suppose so.' He shrugged, his face giving nothing away.

As we walked into reception, Alex was there waiting for us. 'Is she here yet?' I mouthed discreetly to her and she shook her head.

My heart sank, but given Jade's track record, I supposed it wasn't surprising that she was late.

'Let's go through here and I'll show you the contact room,' Alex said to the children.

'Maggie, it's probably best if you stick around until Jade gets here,' she told me quietly.

'Yes, of course.' I nodded.

The girls were soon distracted by the boxes full of toys. Lexie rummaged through the plastic dolls while Amelie looked at a pile of books. Leo sat quietly on the sofa, chewing on his lip nervously.

'Hopefully Mum will be here soon,' I told him, patting his hand for reassurance.

'Yeah, it's fine, she's always late,' he sighed.

Alex went and made us a cup of tea and got the children some beakers of water and a biscuit. We sipped our tea and the girls played, all the while the large clock on the wall ticked away.

Jade was supposed to be have been at the centre at 3.45 p.m. and the contact was supposed to have started at 4 p.m., but by 4.15 p.m. there was still no sign of her.

'I'll just nip out to reception and check that she's on her way,' said Alex, looking stressed.

Thankfully, the girls were too engrossed in the toys to notice that something was wrong, but Leo looked crestfallen.

'She's not coming, is she?' he asked me quietly, suddenly looking very young.

'I don't know, flower,' I said, desperately hoping that he was wrong.

I noticed that he'd peeled the skin off his lip again and it was bleeding so I handed him a tissue.

A few minutes later Alex popped her head around the door.

'Maggie, can I have a quick word?' she asked.

My heart sank.

'Yes, of course,' I replied.

As soon as I stepped outside and saw Alex's face, I knew Leo's instincts were right.

'I tried to ring her twice and it went straight to voicemail,' she sighed. 'Third time she finally picked up. She said she's got a bad headache and she can't come.'

I shook my head. 'Has she been drinking, do you think?'

'She sounded very vague and she was slurring her words,' Alex said.

It wasn't my place to judge parents and I'd never met Jade, but I felt so bitterly disappointed and frustrated for the children.

Why hadn't she cancelled the session earlier, instead of allowing them to come all the way to the contact centre to sit there waiting for her? It was emotional cruelty.

It was gut-wrenching having to tell children that their own parents hadn't bothered to turn up to see them. Little ones shouldn't have to face that kind of rejection.

'We'd better go and break the news,' sighed Alex.

It never got any easier.

When we walked back in the room all three children looked up expectantly. I could tell from Leo's face he already knew what was coming.

'I'm afraid your mum's got a bad headache so she won't be able to come today,' Alex told them. 'But we'll try and arrange for you to see her next week when she's feeling better.'

'I told you,' snapped Leo angrily.

Lexie carried on playing and didn't react.

'Where's Mummy, Leo?' Amelie asked him, looking confused.

It was as if she hadn't registered or believed what Alex was telling her and was looking to Leo for an explanation.

'You heard what Alex said,' he said impatiently. 'She's got a headache so she's not coming.'

'Is she sleeping?' asked Lexie, suddenly piping up.

'Yes,' he said. 'She's asleep.'

'She does sleep lots,' said Lexie, looking unsurprised.

Sadly, the girls seemed to simply accept the news without any fuss, and it was clear they were used to their mother's erratic behaviour. I could see Leo was bitterly disappointed though, and I was absolutely gutted for him that he'd been let down like this.

I knew I needed to get them out of the contact centre and back to my house as quickly as I could.

I didn't say anything about it in the car and all three of them were quiet. When we got home I turned on the television. This was a time when TV was OK, as I thought all three of them needed to zone out and try to switch off from what had just happened.

Even though the girls had seemed to be unfazed by the incident at the conference centre, they were both exhausted when we got home, so I put them to bed early that night. When I came downstairs again, I sat on the sofa with Leo, who was staring at the television half-heartedly.

'How are you doing, lovey?' I asked him. 'You must be so disappointed that you didn't get to see your mum today.'

'She forgets everything. That's why I need to go home to help her remember things.'

I felt so sad for him, and it was horrible to see that he was still making excuses for his mum. At his age he shouldn't feel so responsible for a parent.

Alex rang me the following morning.

'How are the kids doing today?' she asked me.

'They're coping,' I told her. 'The girls seem fine. Leo's taken it a lot harder, but I suppose that's not really surprising given that he's older and more aware of what's going on.'

'How's his eating been?' she asked. 'I know you mentioned you were a bit worried.'

'It's been better, actually,' I said, thinking about it. 'He had a roast on Sunday and fish fingers the other day and I've been giving him money to buy lunch at school.'

'That's good,' she said. 'And is he still wetting the bed every night?'

'I'm afraid so,' I replied. 'I think it's all linked to anxiety.'

After I'd put the phone down to Alex, I realised that I hadn't yet checked Leo's room to see if his sheets needed washing. Normally I'd just check his bed in the mornings after I'd dropped him and Amelie at school and bung the sheets in the wash. It was still early days so I hadn't tried to talk to him about it as I didn't want to embarrass him. The other night I had offered to wake him before I went to bed so he could go to the toilet, but he'd refused and had been mortified at the mere mention of it.

Lexie was happily playing downstairs so I went up to Leo's room to check. As soon as I walked in, the strong scent of ammonia hit my nostrils. The sheets were sodden and as I pulled them off and stripped the duvet, I noticed something tucked down the side of the bed between the mattress and the wall. I put my hand down there and pulled out whatever it was.

It was a supermarket carrier bag and there were two more shoved down the side of the bed with it. Nervously, I opened one up and looked inside. The smell of rotting meat hit my nostrils and I was shocked to find a chicken drumstick, a couple of dried-up roast potatoes and a soggy Yorkshire pudding all wrapped up in a sheet of kitchen roll. I cast my mind back to the roast that I'd made at the weekend and remembered how eagerly Leo had seemed to wolf it down. I opened the other two plastic bags. One had two fish fingers and some peas in it, the other had a half-eaten burger shoved in the bottom. My head spun as I struggled to make sense of it all. Leo had clearly been pretending to eat when he'd been somehow saving his food and hiding it. It was clear that we had a bigger problem on our hands than I ever could have imagined.

SIX

Another Chance

So many thoughts whirred around my head as I stared at the bags of food I'd found hidden in Leo's room. Food that I'd cooked for him and thought that he'd eaten. I'd dismissed my concerns about his weight before, and his eating habits over the past few days had reassured me that everything was OK. It had been a relief as I'd watched him wolf down roast chicken, tuck into fish fingers or a burger. Yet somehow, unbeknown to me, he'd managed to hide most of it rather than actually eating it. I couldn't even imagine how he'd managed it without any of us noticing. All I could think was that he'd shoved it in his pocket or hidden it in his lap when I had been distracted by the girls.

It was common for children in the care system to have issues around food as they'd often come from homes where food was in short supply. I'd fostered countless children who would steal or hoard food, or overeat because they were worried about where their next meal was coming from. I'd also fostered girls who were anorexic, who would refuse point-blank to eat anything, or binge and then make themselves sick after a meal. I'd never come across a boy with an eating disorder though, and I didn't honestly know what to think about Leo. Was this a long-term problem or a temporary reaction to the traumatic week that he'd had?

I was so confused and I felt I needed to talk it through with someone I knew well and could trust, so I called my friend Vicky. She was a single foster carer like me and I knew she was in between placements so I hoped she would be free.

'Have you got time to come round for a chat?' I asked her.

'Yes, of course,' she replied. 'Is everything OK, Maggie?'

'Something's going on with one of my new children and it would really help me to talk it through,' I said.

As a single foster carer, I felt so lucky to have good friends like Vicky and several others who lived nearby. Since Louisa had moved in with Charlie, I really missed having someone to chat to about things. I didn't like to burden Graham with worries about my fostering work.

When Vicky came round half an hour later, Lexie was playing happily with the doll's house, so I put the kettle on and we had a chat. I told her about the bags of food that I'd found hidden in Leo's room.

'That doesn't sound good,' she sighed. 'To be honest, this is a new one for me as well, Maggie.

'I've had girls with issues around food before but not boys.'

I explained that I wasn't sure how to handle it at this stage.

'Am I jumping the gun by labelling this as an eating disorder?' I wondered aloud. 'Am I making an issue where there isn't one?'

Leo had had a turbulent week since he'd been taken into care. He was living in a strange house, he didn't know if his mum was going to get in touch, and to top it all off, he'd been badly let down by her not showing up at contact. That would be enough to make anyone lose their appetite.

'The poor lad doesn't know if he's coming or going,' I sighed. 'Yes, he is very skinny, but perhaps he always has been.'

I still had so many questions, but I felt better now I'd talked things over with Vicky.

'Are you going to say anything to Leo?' she asked before she left.

'I think I have to,' I said. 'Apart from anything else, it's unhygienic having bags of rotting food in his room. And of course I'll discuss my concerns with his social worker and see what she thinks.'

'Good luck,' said Vicky. 'The poor lad's obviously having a hard time of things.'

He certainly was, and I didn't know how he was going to react when I tried to talk to him about it. When he got in from school that afternoon, the girls were in the living room and he was in the kitchen getting his homework out of his school bag. I didn't want to sit him down and make a big deal out of it as I knew that would put too much pressure on him and was likely to make him clam up altogether.

'Leo, I found some bags of food in your bedroom today,' I told him casually. 'You can't keep food in your room, flower, because it will go rotten and make the room smell.'

His cheeks flushed red and he continued to rummage through his bag.

'Leo, no one's forcing you to eat,' I told him gently. 'If you don't want the food I make for you, we can talk about giving you something else that you will eat, but you can't go around hiding it.'

I paused and waited for his reaction. I expected him to leap on the defensive, to deny it all and protest that it hadn't been him, which was usually the position taken by teenagers. I was surprised to see that he looked mortified and was close to tears.

'OK,' he mumbled, fiddling with the hem of his school shirt.

'It's all right, lovey,' I continued. 'If there's a problem, we can talk about it and try to sort it out.'

'There isn't a problem,' he snapped, storming out of the kitchen and stomping upstairs.

I left it there. I didn't want to upset him and I'd said all I needed to say.

While he was upstairs, I gave Alex a call as I knew I needed to update her. I told her about what I'd found and the conversation that I'd just had with Leo.

'I don't honestly know where to go from here,' I sighed.

I explained that I didn't know whether his reluctance to eat was about stress and anxiety, or even whether it was because I was making different kinds of food to what he was used to.

'Obviously, something like this is worrying,' Alex told me when I'd finished. 'But all we can do is a keep an eye on it for now and then further down the line we can make a decision about whether we think it's a temporary re-action to what's been going on, or a long-term problem that needs addressing.

'We can talk about it at the professionals meeting next week and get his school's view.'

I couldn't help but feel stressed that night as I served up dinner. I was worried about whether Leo was going to eat the spaghetti Bolognese that I was about to put in front of him, but I also knew that he was going to be very conscious of me watching him and I didn't want him to feel under any extra pressure. I'd already moved the carrier bags from the kitchen drawer into a high cupboard and I'd deliberately given him a small portion so as not to overwhelm him.

'Leo, why have you only got a little plate like me?' asked Lexie as she sat down at the table.

He went red. 'I'm just not that hungry today,' he said to her.

'There's lots left if anybody wants more,' I said casually as I sat down.

Even though I did my best to hide it, I watched Leo like a hawk to make sure he was actually chewing and swallowing the food and not squirrelling it away into a tissue or in his lap. He ate very slowly and pushed his pasta around the plate a lot, but I was relieved to see that he ate it.

Over the next few days, I checked Leo's room every morning when he was at school. Much to my relief, I didn't find any more hidden bags of food. I was still watching him at the dinner table, but as far as I could tell, he seemed to be eating OK. I was still giving him small portions, but at least he was finishing it all. On Alex's advice, I was also making him milky drinks and offering him puddings in a bid to try and boost his calorie intake.

He was still wetting the bed most nights. I could tell he was ashamed about it as he'd started stripping the bed when his sheets were wet and putting them in the laundry basket rather than waiting for me to find them. One morning, I went to check to see if his sheets were there so I could put them in the wash. I fished out something white, assuming it was a pillow case, but I was surprised to find that it was one of Leo's school shirts. As I put it back in, I noticed a large reddy-brown stain on the lower front part of it. My heart started thumping. I knew instantly it was blood.

Where had that come from? Had he hurt himself or been in a fight?

When Leo got home that night after school, I asked him about the blood on his school shirt. He wouldn't look at me.

'Oh – erm, I was trying to get the football and I crawled under a fence to get it and scraped my front,' he told me.

'Do you want me to have a look at it for you?' I asked him. 'It must be deep to have bled that much?'

'No, don't worry,' he said. 'A teacher put a plaster on it for me.'

I had to believe what he was telling me. As he was older, I couldn't demand that he lifted up his shirt and showed me the cut if he didn't want to, but I made a mental note to myself to keep an eye on it and check in with Leo that it was healing.

A few days later, it was time for the professionals meeting. Vicky had kindly agreed to come to my house and look after Lexie while I went to the meeting at Social Services. Everyone involved in the children's care would be there, from Alex and her manager, a man called Richard, Miss Hughes from Amelie's school and one of Leo's teachers, as well as Becky and myself. Jade, the children's mother, had also been invited along. I was both a little bit intrigued and slightly nervous to meet her. Foster carers often got a frosty reception from birth parents as we were the ones who were looking after their children instead of them, and as hard as it could sometimes be, I'd been working as a foster carer long enough to understand that it wasn't personal.

'I hope it goes well,' Vicky told me as I got ready to leave.

'Thanks.' I smiled. 'It will be good for all of us to have more of a long-term plan in place.'

When I got there, Alex was making everyone a hot drink.

'They'll all in the meeting room,' she told me, gesturing down the corridor.

'Is Jade here?' I asked.

She shook her head.

'Not yet,' she sighed. 'And given her track record, I'm not sure she's going to turn up at all.'

We all assembled in one of the rooms. Ten minutes after the scheduled start time, Jade still wasn't there so the decision was made to start without her.

Alex's manager Richard was leading the meeting. He was a small, slight man in his forties. He was new to Social Services and I hadn't worked with him before so he introduced himself to everyone. He described how the children had come into the care system and then he turned to me.

'Maggie, can you give us an update on how the children are now?' he asked.

I told everyone how well the girls had settled in.

'On the face of it, they seem largely unaffected by what's happened,' I said. 'But I think that's because they've still got their main care-giver with them.'

'Who's that?' asked Richard, looking puzzled.

'Leo,' I explained. 'From everything I've seen, the girls depend on him like they would a parent. They look to him for comfort and reassurance and I think he's been responsible for looking after both of them for quite some time.'

'And what about Leo?' questioned Richard. 'How does he seem?'

'As if he's got the weight of the world on his shoulders,' I sighed. 'He's very anxious and has repeatedly asked that he and his sisters be allowed to go home to their mum.'

I talked through my worries about Leo, and explained about his bed-wetting as well as his low weight, his reluctance to eat and the hidden food I'd found in his bedroom.

'Did the consultant who did his LAC medical think there was an issue with his weight?' asked Richard.

'Unfortunately, Leo refused to allow the medical to take place, so he hasn't been examined,' I sighed.

Leo's form tutor from his secondary school, Mrs Collins, had come to the meeting.

'I can ask the dinner supervisors to keep an eye on him at lunchtimes to check that he's eating something if that would help?' she suggested.

She described how Leo's attendance had been poor over the past few months but that when he was in school, he was quiet and diligent.

'What about friendship groups?' asked Richard.

The teacher shrugged.

'He talks to people and seems to be well liked by his classmates, but he generally keeps himself to himself and doesn't have a specific close friend or group of friends,' she said.

Miss Hughes also told the meeting how Amelie had often been picked up and dropped off at school by Leo.

Alex then explained the situation with the children's mother, Jade.

'Jade's currently in a relationship with a man called Tyrone,' she said. 'It seems to be a volatile relationship and records show the neighbours have called the police a couple of times as they were worried for her safety. I've also seen her with bruises and a black eye.'

She also described how one of the main concerns was Jade's drinking and how she'd failed to turn up for contact last week. I felt sad hearing it all spoken out loud.

'Hearing all of this, combined with the fact that Jade hasn't turned up today, I think we need to start the process of getting an interim care order,' said Richard. 'Until more questions are answered, it's clear the children need to stay in Maggie's care. Let's also see how the next contact session goes.'

Alex and I stayed behind after the meeting to have a chat.

She explained she had arranged to meet Jade at the contact centre in a couple of days' time.

'If she does turn up, I'll give you a call and you can bring the children straight up to see her,' she told me. 'But please don't mention anything to them until we know that she's definitely there.'

'Of course,' I said.

Neither of us wanted them to have to go through a repeat of what they had the other day.

On the afternoon the contact had been scheduled for, I picked up Amelie from school as normal and Leo came back shortly afterwards. As I had promised Alex, I didn't mention anything to the children about it, and to be honest, I wasn't holding out much hope of Jade turning up at all.

When my phone rang, I was surprised to see Alex's number.

'Hi, Maggie, Jade's arrived at the contact centre, so it'd be great if you could bring the kids down now.'

'No problem – I'll let them know and we'll head straight over to you,' I told her.

All three were watching TV in the living room together.

'Alex has just rung to say your mum's at the contact centre and she'd really like to see you,' I told them. 'So if you all get your shoes on, we can get in the car and go.'

The girls looked surprised but quickly jumped up off the sofa, chattering excitedly to each other.

Leo remained sitting there, looking stony-faced.

'Come on, Leo,' Lexie said, grabbing his hand and trying to pull him up. 'Let's go and see Mummy.'

But he didn't move an inch.

'Girls, why don't you go and get your shoes on while I talk to Leo,' I told them.

They ran out into the hallway.

'What is it, lovey?' I asked him gently. 'Don't you want to go and see your mum?'

'You're wasting your time,' he sighed. 'She won't turn up again.'

'No, Leo, your mum is there right now with Alex waiting for you,' I reassured him. 'You haven't got to worry about her not turning up this time because she's already there.'

'Really?' he asked in disbelief.

'Honestly,' I said.

Leo still didn't look convinced.

'All right,' he sighed. 'Let's go.'

'Are you sure you're OK about this?' I asked him.

'Yeah.' He nodded.

But his body language seemed to suggest the complete opposite. I could see the worry and apprehension in his eyes and, above all, he looked absolutely terrified.

SEVEN

On the Attack

As we walked in, Alex was waiting for us in reception.

'Is our mummy really here?' Lexie grinned. 'Can we see her now?'

'Yes, I'll take you through to the contact room in a second,' Alex told her.

While the two girls were holding hands and jumping around excitedly, Leo hung back. Alex must have noticed how apprehensive he was.

'Are you OK, Leo?' she asked him.

He chewed on his lip anxiously and looked at me, his eyes full of worry.

'Can you come into the room with us?' he asked me in a quiet voice.

I turned to Alex. It wasn't normal practice for a foster carer to sit in on the contact with the children unless they or the biological parents had asked.

'Yes, of course.' She nodded. 'Maggie can go in with you if you want.'

73

I gave her an appreciative smile.

'Right then, let's go and see your mum,' she told the kids.

We followed her down a long corridor to the contact room. The girls quickly pushed open the door and ran in. Leo hesitated and I could see him stiffen up.

'Shall we go in and see Mum, Leo?' Alex asked him cheerfully.

He nodded and trudged through the door, still looking reluctant.

I had to admit that I was curious to meet Jade. When we walked in, she was sitting on the sofa. She was small with long bleached blonde hair, with dark brown, almost black, roots and she was wearing a pink hoodie, jeans and scruffy white trainers. Her eyes were bloodshot and there were dark shadows underneath them and she looked very pale. She smelt of an overpowering mix of body spray and nicotine. She couldn't have been any older than late twenties, which meant she must have had Leo when she was still at school.

'Jade, this is Maggie,' Alex told her. 'She's the children's foster carer.'

'Pleased to meet you.' I smiled.

Jade didn't say a word. She just flashed me a look of disdain as if I was something that she'd stepped on in the street.

The girls ran straight over to her, beaming, Lexie's arms stretched out wide.

'Mummy, you're awake.' Amelie smiled.

'Course I'm awake, stupid,' Jade snapped.

Lexie climbed onto her lap and Amelie sat next to her and started twiddling her hair.

'Oh, girls, give over,' Jade sighed, lifting Lexie off her and batting Amelie away. 'I can't cope with you climbing all over me and you're doing my head in pulling on my hair like that, Amelie. I've just washed it.'

The girls looked disappointed by their mum's lack of interest, but they soon gave up trying to get her attention and it wasn't long before they were distracted by the contents of the toy box in the opposite corner of the room.

While all this had been going on, Leo was standing silently in the corner with his back pressed up against the wall. He and his mum hadn't even acknowledged each other yet.

Jade looked over at him.

'All right, Leo,' she said.

'Leo, why don't you go over and sit with your mum?' Alex suggested.

'Yeah, I'm not going to bite,' laughed Jade.

Reluctantly he perched himself on the opposite end of the sofa, as far away as possible from where his mum was sitting. There were a couple of office chairs there so Alex and I sat down on them.

'Are you all right, Mum?' Leo asked her eventually in a quiet voice.

Jade paused.

'No, Leo,' she sighed. 'I'm not bloody all right. And do you know why?'

He looked down at the floor and shrugged.

'Because the Social have taken away my kids,' she snapped. 'And do you know why they've taken my kids?'

I suddenly started to feel very uneasy about where this conversation was heading and I shifted in my chair.

'Because of you,' sneered Jade. 'All of this mess is your fault. You cocked up. Why couldn't you have just done what you were told and pick up Amelie from school, then we wouldn't be here.'

I knew I couldn't just sit there and let Jade lay into Leo like this. We had to say something. Luckily, it was clear from Alex's face that she felt the same way.

'Jade, I need to stop you there,' she told her firmly. 'This isn't an appropriate conversation for you to be having with Leo. I will have to stop the session if you continue,' she warned her.

Jade rolled her eyes.

I was pleased that Alex had intervened and not me. As the children's foster carer, I wasn't even officially supposed to be in the session, so I didn't feel that it was really my place to wade in.

'Leo, why don't you tell your mum how school's going?' Alex suggested, desperately trying to change the subject.

But Leo's mind was still firmly on what his mum had said to him.

'I'm sorry, Mum,' he whimpered, his head hung. 'I tried to pick up Amelie, but the school wouldn't let me. They said it needed to be you.'

'Oh, don't be giving me your excuses, Leo,' she snapped. 'You messed up and you know it.'

I was taken aback hearing Jade attacking Leo like this. She hadn't seen her children for almost two weeks and yet here she was picking a row with her son and ignoring her little girls. I looked over to where Lexie and Amelie were playing in the corner. Thankfully, they were so engrossed in the toys, they seemed oblivious to what was going on over this side of the room.

Alex jumped in straight away.

'Jade, this is your last warning,' she told her. 'As I said before, change the subject please or this session is coming to an end.'

Jade looked furious and she turned on Alex, her face red.

'Don't you tell me what I can and can't talk to my son about,' she ranted. 'He's my kid and I can talk to him however I want. The only reason why you're f*****g involved is because of him.'

I fiddled with my bracelet, nervously. Jade was getting more and more aggressive and I didn't like it at all. Every bone in my body was telling me to get these children out of the room, but I knew I had to follow Alex's guidance. I looked over at the girls – thankfully they were still engrossed in playing with the toys.

'It's not Leo's fault that Social Services are involved, but as I have said, that's not a conversation we should be having here,' replied Alex.

'Well I disagree,' spat Jade.

Leo sat there, frozen to the spot, looking absolutely distraught.

'I'm sorry, Mum,' he whimpered. 'But all of this happened because of you and your drinking and because you were too out of it to collect Amelie.'

Out of nowhere, and before any of us could stop her, Jade reared up out of her seat like an angry tiger, lunged towards Leo and slapped him hard across the face.

Crack.

The sound echoed around the room.

'Oh my God,' I gasped.

Leo sat there, stunned, his hand clasped to his cheek, which had immediately turned a bright shade of red.

Alex leapt up and went over to Jade to make sure she didn't try anything else. 'This contact session is ending right now,' she said sharply.

While Alex was restraining Jade, I knew I needed to get the children out of the contact room as quickly as I could.

'Come on, flower,' I told Leo, quietly, hurrying over to him.

I went to put my arm around his shoulders and I could feel him shaking. As he stood up, he looked down at himself and shuddered in horror. There was a large wet patch on the crotch of his jeans. The poor boy must have wet himself with the shock.

Unfortunately, Jade had noticed too.

'Oh no, your brother's pissed himself,' she laughed to the girls. 'I thought he'd have grown out of being a pissy pants now he's a teenager but obviously not.'

Leo's cheeks burned red and he looked totally and utterly mortified.

'That's enough, Jade,' snapped Alex.

I was utterly horrified that she was being so cruel. I knew I needed to get Leo out of that room and far away from her as quickly as I could. I rounded up the girls who looked puzzled at why the session was over so soon.

'Time to go,' I said, ushering them out towards the door.

'But that wasn't very long,' sighed Amelie, looking confused.

'At least you've seen Mummy now,' I said.

I led them straight out of the building. Leo still hadn't said a word as we marched across the car park to the car. He was like a zombie, staring into space.

'Leo, you sit in the front with me,' I told him gently as I unlocked the car.

I always keep a stash of blankets in my car for the kids, so I got one out of the back for him and put it down on the front passenger seat.

'Sit on this, sweetie,' I told him.

He looked so embarrassed as he sat down on the blanket and wrapped it self-consciously around his lap to hide his wet jeans. I put my hand on his shoulder to try and offer him some little bit of comfort.

'Leo, I'm so sorry that this has happened,' I said to him gently. 'None of this is your fault, and your mum was wrong to slap you.'

He hung his head and looked like he was about to burst into tears.

'Let's get you home,' I sighed.

I breathed a sigh of relief as we drove out of the contact centre car park and far away from Jade and the risk of any more run-ins. I was so angry and outraged about what had happened. How could she treat her own child like that? How could she humiliate him, berate him and belittle him, especially after he'd been taken into care? Her cruelty was astounding and to do all that in front of a social worker and foster carer was unbelievable.

As we drove along, Leo still looked shell-shocked and didn't say a word. I didn't push him to talk; instead, I chit-chatted to the girls, who were talking to each other about some TV programme they liked.

When we pulled up outside the house, I turned to him.

'As soon as we get in, flower, why don't you go and get yourself a shower?' I said gently. 'Just put your clothes in the wash and I'll sort them out.'

He nodded. He did what I'd asked while I sorted the girls out with a snack. He came down half an hour later in clean clothes.

'What do you want to do?' I asked him. 'Do you want to come into the kitchen with me and help me make dinner?'

He shook his head.

'I just want to watch telly,' he mumbled.

He looked exhausted and I was happy for him to do whatever he wanted. At this point I didn't want to push him to talk about what happened. While the girls and Leo were in the front room, I quickly popped upstairs and got Leo's clothes to put in the washing machine. I didn't want him to see them and be reminded of what had happened.

While I was in the kitchen making dinner, Alex rang.

'I'm so sorry about contact, Maggie,' she sighed. 'I'd got no idea Jade was going to go off on one like that. It was just horrendous. How's Leo doing?'

'No, me neither,' I said. 'Leo's been very quiet and I think he's still in shock. He's had a shower and I've just left him to watch TV,' I continued. 'He's not even in a fit state to be able to talk about it at the moment so I'm just carrying on as normal.'

'Poor boy,' replied Alex. 'I think that's all you can do.'

It just felt like one huge mess.

'So what's going to happen now, after everything that happened today?' I asked Alex.

'I need to speak to my manager ASAP,' she told me. 'To all intents and purposes, what Jade did to Leo today was assault. I also need to talk to Leo about it and then we need to decide whether to get the police involved.'

I wasn't sure if that would help anyone, but I understood that Social Services were within their rights to do it.

Alex explained that they wouldn't organise another contact session until some work had been done with Jade to make sure that she wouldn't react like that again and they could guarantee the safety of the children.

'It might be that we decide to do separate contact sessions,' she explained. 'So the girls would see Mum on their own, and Leo would have his own session.'

I'd been in contact sessions before where parents had been classed as volatile, so it would be done in a room with a table, with the parents sitting on one side and the child on the other. There would be contact workers or social workers on both sides to ensure that there was a physical barrier between parents and their child so they couldn't physically reach each other.

'Jade was OK with the girls,' I said. 'If anything, she just seemed disinterested in them.'

'I'll see what my manager thinks,' agreed Alex. 'Let's see how Leo is tomorrow and don't send him to school if you don't think he's ready. He's been through a lot today.'

He certainly had. Alex and I agreed to catch up the following day.

At dinner time, Leo was still very quiet. He sat there in silence, pushing the cottage pie around his plate. Even though I was concerned about his eating, I wasn't going to force him into eating anything tonight. He was stressed and upset and I understood if he wasn't hungry.

'Listen, lovey, if you don't feel like eating dinner, then don't worry,' I told him gently. 'I can always do you some toast later if you change your mind.'

'I'm not hungry,' he told me, looking relieved.

That night, after I'd put the girls to bed, I made Leo a hot chocolate and went and sat with him on the sofa. Even though he might not be up for talking, I still felt I needed to acknowledge what he had been through today.

'Are you OK, lovey?' I asked him gently. 'How are you feeling after everything that happened with your mum today? I was really shocked by what happened, and I'm so sorry you had to go through that.'

He shrugged.

'I tried really hard to do what she wanted, but they wouldn't let me take Amelie from school,' he whispered, his eyes filling up with tears.

'Leo, it's not your fault,' I told him, putting my arm around his shoulders to try and comfort him. 'Your sisters are not your responsibility. You're a child. Your mum shouldn't have spoken to you like that and she certainly shouldn't have slapped you.'

It was unbelievable that Jade was unwilling to take any blame herself and was projecting it all onto Leo. I couldn't understand how anyone could act like that, and to make it worse, she'd done it in front of her social worker. Did she not even want her children back?

I didn't want to push Leo too much or force him to talk any more because I could see that he was drained.

'It's your bedtime now, flower,' I told him gently.

I was worried that he would be too upset to sleep but to my relief, when I checked on him fifteen minutes later, he was out like a light.

I felt shattered too, but I think I was still in shock after what had happened. When I went downstairs, I decided to give Graham a call. I missed Louisa being around and the house felt so quiet.

'Are you OK?' he asked. 'You sound upset.'

'It's just been a long day,' I sighed. 'I had a difficult contact session with the kids and their mum and to be honest it really got to me.'

'You'll feel better after a good sleep,' he told me. 'Tomorrow is another day.'

'That's usually my line,' I laughed. 'I'm always telling the kids that.'

But I knew he was right. Hopefully things would start to get better for Leo because they certainly couldn't get any worse.

EIGHT

The Hardest Conversation

A week had passed since the awful contact session that had ended so abruptly. Seven long days that Alex had spent trying and failing to get hold of Jade.

'I don't know what I can do,' she'd told me despairingly on the phone. 'I've been round to the flat, I've rung, I've sent letters and emails, but Jade is obviously avoiding me.'

We were back to square one again. Also none of the children had asked about their mother. Leo had been extremely quiet and he hadn't wanted to talk about anything to do with Jade or the contact session.

Finally, ten days after the contact session, Alex came to see me. She seemed very subdued and I could see there was something bothering her. Leo and Amelie were at school and Lexie was playing in the living room.

'Are you OK?' I asked. 'Come into the kitchen and I'll put the kettle on.'

I'd always been struck by what a dynamic and upbeat person

84

Alex seemed, but today she looked as if she'd got the weight of the world on her shoulders.

'Well, I finally got hold of Jade,' she told me, sitting down wearily at the kitchen table. 'She actually let me into the flat and we had a cup of tea.'

'Thank goodness,' I breathed, feeling relieved. 'That's great news, isn't it?'

Alex shook her head. 'Not exactly,' she sighed.

Alex explained that they'd talked about how the last contact session had gone and how next time it would need to be done differently to protect Leo.

'I said that before she could see the kids again, Social Services would need to do some work with her to make sure we didn't have another repeat of the last session. I also explained that we're applying for an interim care order to keep the children in care while all of this is going on, and that she'd probably need to start a parenting assessment before we could think about returning the children to her care.'

'How did she take that?' I asked.

Alex looked downcast.

'You're not going to believe this, Maggie,' she sighed. 'She swore at me and told me in no uncertain terms to stuff it. Her exact words were that she wasn't prepared to jump through any more hoops because she doesn't want her kids back anyway.'

I was shocked.

'She actually said that?' I gasped. 'Surely she doesn't mean it and it's just a knee-jerk reaction?'

'I don't think so,' replied Alex, shaking her head sadly. 'She asked if there was something that she could sign there and then because she was so sure that she didn't want them back.'

It was unbelievable.

'Are you going to give her time to reconsider?' I asked.

Alex nodded. 'I said I'd give her a couple of days to think about it, although she was adamant she wouldn't change her mind. She told me she couldn't be bothered with Social Services any more and just wants to move on with her life.'

I'd seen it happen before and I knew it would happen again, but I still found it shocking when parents weren't willing to fight for their children and decided they didn't want them back. It happened for a lot of reasons. Parents might suddenly have free time again and realise that life is a lot easier without the responsibility of children, or they might just get sick of having social workers checking up on them and putting their lives under a microscope. I always found it a bitter pill to swallow and it horrified me that adults were able to hand over their children like they were nothing more than an unwanted parcel.

'But what's going to happen now? I asked her. 'And how on earth are we going to tell the kids?'

'Let's not decide anything until I've spoken to Jade in a couple of days,' Alex told me. 'You never know, she might have a change of heart.'

Over the next two days, I tried to put my conversation with Alex to the back of my mind, but it was impossible. Every time I looked at Amelie, Lexie and Leo, I felt myself welling up at the thought of what we might have to tell them. I couldn't help but worry about how they would deal with that level of rejection. The girls were very resilient; they'd settled well into their new routine at my house and they were chatty little things. They were sleeping and eating and as long as Leo was by their side, they were OK. It was him that I was so worried about.

To be honest, I was dreading Alex's call, and when her number appeared on my screen a couple of days later, I felt sick. I knew immediately by the despondent tone of her voice what the answer was.

'I'm afraid Jade's not changed her mind,' she told me. 'My manager's keen for us to go for a full care order as soon as we can.'

'It's just all so sudden,' I sighed.

'I know it's hard for us to accept, but I really do think it's what she wants, Maggie,' Alex told me. 'We can't force her to fight for her kids. She wasn't drunk either of the times we talked and she was very clear about it.

'She told me things had been easier with Tyrone since the children had been taken into care. The kids got on Tyrone's nerves and she said they were a hassle for both of them.'

'That's heartbreaking,' I sighed.

I always tried not to judge birth parents and their decisions as I didn't know what they'd been through in their own lives. But I found Jade's reasons hard to swallow: she was basically saying that her children were an inconvenience, and she'd chosen her boyfriend over them.

'To be frank, Maggie, I'm shocked too,' Alex told me. 'They're lovely children. But what's important now is that we try to secure their future and come up with a long-term plan.'

'What about the children's dads?' I asked Alex. 'Or are there any grandparents or other family members who might be worth considering?'

'I did ask,' she said. 'But there's no one around. Jade's mum died when she was a teenager and she doesn't see her dad. She's not in touch with Leo or the girls' dads either. She said she didn't even put their names on the birth certificates.'

I knew that Alex would be feeling just as frustrated as I was. However, she kept her tone professional and was clearly focused on sorting out the practical elements.

'Maggie, I haven't checked it out with Becky at your agency yet, but are you happy to keep fostering them until we've got a long-term plan in place?' she asked me.

'Yes, of course,' I replied, without hesitation.

After everything the children had been through, and with this new shocking development, I was keen to give them as much stability as possible.

'Does Jade want to say goodbye to them?' I asked.

Often, when a child was going into care permanently, a last contact session was arranged so children and parents could say goodbye to each other. No matter how hard or painful it is, I believe that it is important for children to have that closure and to put an end to any fantasy that one day their parent might come back for them.

'She said no,' said Alex, sounding upset. 'As far as she's concerned, she saw the kids the other week and that's that.'

I couldn't believe it. While I knew that lots of people's situations made it difficult for them to care for their children, I couldn't understand how someone could just turn their back on their children after thirteen years of parenting.

I couldn't help but worry about what impact not saying goodbye to Jade would have on the children, especially Leo. His last visit with his mum had been so traumatic for him. Jade had been angry with him and that was going to be his lasting memory of her.

'Alex, how on earth are we going to tell them?' I sighed, the weight of what she'd told me starting to sink in.

It was the hardest conversation in the world to have. There was no good way to tell a child that their parents didn't want them any more. As hard as it would be on Amelie and Lexie, at least they weren't old enough to fully understand their mother's rejection of them. But Leo wasn't a child; he was a teenager, and no matter how we tried to dress it up, he was going to understand the reality. His self-esteem was already so fragile and his anxiety level was high. How would he cope with yet another rejection?

'Because of their ages, I think we should tell the girls separately,' Alex told me. 'We'll need to phrase it very simply and in a way that they understand. It's going to be hard, but I think we need to be upfront with Leo and be honest about the situation.'

'I think Leo needs to be there when you tell the girls,' I suggested. 'They always look to him for reassurance.'

The thought of telling the children made me feel sick, but both Alex and I knew that it needed to be done. As their social worker, it was Alex's responsibility to tell them, but I wanted to be there to support all three of them.

Alex and I decided that it would be best if she came round to my house that afternoon when the children got home from school. My stomach churned with nerves as I prepared them a snack.

'Alex is coming round in a little while to talk to you,' I mentioned casually as I handed them a drink of water.

Leo nodded in acknowledgement, but the girls didn't react as by now they were used to Alex popping round. They were both playing in the living room when she arrived, and Leo was in the kitchen with me doing his homework.

'Leo, can you, me and Maggie have a chat?' Alex asked as walked in.

'Do you want me to go and get my sisters?' he replied, looking up from his homework.

Alex flashed me a look.

'No, flower, I think Alex is going to talk to you on your own first and then speak to the girls afterwards,' I told him.

As we sat down at the kitchen table, Leo suddenly looked on edge, and he seemed to sense that something important was coming.

'What's happened?' he asked anxiously, his eyes wide. 'Is it my mum? Is she OK?'

My heart broke for him. Even after everything that had happened and the callous way Jade had treated him, he was still concerned about her. If only the feeling was mutual.

'She's fine, Leo,' Alex reassured him. 'I saw her today and we had a long talk about what was going to happen in the future with you and your sisters.'

I could feel my heart pounding in my chest. I looked down at my hands and fiddled nervously with my watch as Alex continued to talk.

'Your mum's thought about it really, really hard but, unfortunately, she doesn't feel that she's able to look after you and Lexie and Amelie any more,' she told him gently. 'She feels it's best for the three of you to remain in the care system.'

Leo hesitated. Then his face crumped with anger.

'Why don't you just say it?' he yelled. 'She's giving us up, isn't she? She doesn't want us any more. She's more interested in that Tyrone than us.'

Leo was thirteen. No matter how harsh the truth was, we owed it to him to be honest. He knew his own mother better than anyone and would see through any attempts to sugar-coat the situation.

'I'm so sorry, Leo,' I told him. 'I know it's a really, really hard thing for you to accept but sadly your mum feels that she can't be a parent to you or your sisters any more.'

He shook his head. 'But that's not fair,' he cried. 'I tried my hardest, I really did.'

'Sweetie, it's not your fault,' I told him, desperately wishing I could make him believe it.

I reached across the table to hold his hand but he angrily shook me off.

'Will we ever see her again?' he asked in a quiet voice.

Alex shook her head.

'I'm afraid your mum doesn't feel able to have contact with you or your sisters again.'

Leo banged the table with his fist. Hot, furious tears slid down his face as the enormity of what we were saying slowly started to sink in. He was angry and hurting, and his pain was palpable. It was almost unbearable to witness.

'Leo, I know you must be hurting so much, but I'm going to need your help,' Alex told him gently. 'Do you think you can help me tell your sisters what I've just told you? Because they're only little, it's going to be really hard for them to understand.'

I put my hand on his shoulder.

'They'll be OK,' he said bravely, wiping his face. 'They've got me so they'll be all right and they like being at Maggie's house.'

I smiled. 'They're very lucky girls to have a brother like you,' I told him.

I went and got the girls and brought them into the kitchen.

Lexie was very fidgety and wouldn't sit still, but Amelie looked like she was listening as Alex began to speak.

'I've been talking to your mummy lots today, and she's decided that it's best that you stay at Maggie's house because she doesn't feel that she's able to look after you any more,' she told them gently.

Lexie had wriggled down from her chair onto the floor by now but Amelie looked deep in thought.

'I saw my mummy the other day,' she pondered. 'But when will I see her next time? Leo, will we have to go to that special place to see her? That room with the toys and the books?'

Leo shook his head sadly. I wasn't sure if Alex was going to answer, but she paused and let Leo speak.

'There's not going to be a next time, Am,' he told her seriously. 'We're not going to see Mummy again or live with her any more.'

'Not ever?' Amelie asked, her blue eyes wide with surprise.

He shook his head. 'Not ever.'

'But will we still see you?' she asked anxiously. 'Will you still be here?'

'Course I will, silly.' Leo smiled. 'I'm always going to be here. And we'll all stay together, OK?'

'OK.' Amelie nodded, looking relieved.

That seemed to be enough to reassure her and before long both she and Lexie were sitting on the floor playing a game of Jenga with Leo.

Alex and I went into the living room to talk.

'That must be one of the worst parts of my job,' she sighed.

'Well, at least it's done now,' I said sympathetically.

'I think it's going to take a while for the girls to fully understand the implications of what we've just told them,' she said.

'It's probably better that way,' I sighed. 'It's Leo I really feel for.'

For thirteen years Jade had been his sole parent. He'd done his best for her and tried his hardest to keep their little family together. I couldn't imagine how hard it must be for him to realise that Jade didn't want to be his mother any more.

'Yes, we'll need to keep a close eye on Leo. I just don't know how he's going to cope with this,' Alex agreed.

'I know,' I replied. 'I'm not going to force him to talk to me, but I'll let him know that I'm here if he needs me or to answer any questions.'

I could see Alex felt as down as I did about what had happened today.

'I don't think I'll ever understand how a mother or father can walk away from their children like that,' I sighed.

'Well, I wonder if perhaps Jade is doing this because she knows she wouldn't pass any parenting assessment? Maybe she feels she's actually doing her best for her children by not prolonging it?' suggested Alex. 'Maybe she genuinely believes that the kids are better off without her, and the best thing she can do for them is to let them go.'

I'd never ever thought of it like that before and it really made me think.

'That's a really positive way of looking at a horrendous situation,' I told her. 'I might even suggest that to Leo later.'

None of us would ever know if it was true or not, but if it gave him some small comfort, it was worth it.

'Maggie, I'll be in touch,' Alex added, gathering up her bag. 'We'll start the paperwork for the care order today and then we'll need to start thinking about a long-term plan. Thanks for your support today.'

'That's OK.' I smiled. 'Thank you for yours.'

When Alex had gone, I went to check on the children. The girls were still in the kitchen playing but there was no sign of Leo.

'Where's your brother?' I asked them.

They just shrugged and carried on with their game.

I went upstairs to Leo's room and knocked on his door. When I pushed it open, he was sitting on his bed staring into space.

'How are you feeling, lovey?' I asked him gently.

'I don't think she ever loved me,' he said, his voice flat. 'Maybe she loved the girls but not me.'

He looked up at me, his eyes filled with tears. 'Why did she bother having us if she didn't want us, Maggie?' he asked.

I went and sat on the bed next to him and wrapped my arms around him.

'I know this is so hard and so sad, flower. But maybe your mum has realised that she can't give you and your sisters the care that you need. Maybe this is her way of doing her best for the three of you because she loves you and wants you all to be happy.'

Leo shook his head sadly. 'No, she's doing what's best for her and Tyrone,' he scoffed. 'It's only ever about her. She doesn't care about me or Am or Lexie at all.'

He sounded far older than his thirteen years, and it was heart-breaking to hear him talking about his mum's failings so frankly.

'As you get older, Leo, you'll realise that adults sometimes behave in ways that we don't understand,' I told him.

He nodded sadly.

'What's going to happen to us?' he asked suddenly, looking panicked. 'Will we stay here?'

'Yes, for now you and your sisters will stay here with me, while Alex and Social Services work out what's best for you all. Is that OK with you?'

'Yeah,' he said, drying his eyes. 'I like it here.'

'Good,' I told him. 'Now let's go down and see your sisters.'

The girls hadn't said anything else about their mum, but for the rest of the evening, I could see they were very clingy with Leo. They kept running up to him and touching his knee or arm.

'Leo's here!' they shouted before running off again.

'What on earth are they doing?' I asked him.

'They used to get scared sometimes when Mum went out at night and left us, so I used to get a blanket and play peekaboo. I'd peep out and tell them I was there to make them feel better. They were a lot littler then, but maybe they're remembering that.'

The girls hadn't asked any questions about their mother or what Alex had said, but I knew it took longer for things to sink in with children of that age. The girls knew their mummy had gone because she wasn't there, but Leo was and he looked after them. They'd never really shown much distress about coming into the care system in the first place. Although they'd briefly craved the familiarity of their old surroundings, neither of the girls had shown any sign of missing their mother. I felt certain that they would be OK because, no matter what happened, their source of comfort hadn't gone. Leo was their security and stability and he was still there.

Leo was the one that I was really worried about. How would this traumatised boy cope with this on top of everything else he'd been through?

NINE

Rock Bottom

EastEnders was on the telly, but to be honest I wasn't paying any attention to it. All I could think about was Lexie, Amelie and Leo and how they had taken the news that we'd told them today. Thankfully, the girls seemed fine when I put them to bed that night.

'Can you read *The Gruffalo* to us?' Lexie had asked cheerfully.

They'd both happily snuggled up together on the bottom bunk and joined in as I read them their favourite book. I thought they might be clingy or tearful, but there were no signs at all that we'd just told them some life-changing news about their biological mummy. Although they were still very young, I knew the implications of their mother's decision might affect the girls for months or even years down the line. My immediate worry was very much for Leo.

He'd been very stoic and brave that evening and had done his best to reassure the girls, but I also knew how deeply he was hurting and how devastating his mum's decision was. When the girls went to bed, he'd taken himself to his bedroom to read his book. I wanted to give him a little bit of time on his own just to sit with his thoughts to try and digest everything that had happened, but by 9 p.m. I decided to go upstairs and check on him. I knew he would probably be shattered, both emotionally and physically, after today, and I wanted him to turn his light out and at least try and get some rest.

I crept upstairs so as not to wake the girls. Thankfully, when I looked in on them they were both fast asleep, clutching their favourite rag dolls.

Then I went to check on Leo. I could see under the door that his light was on so I assumed he was still awake. I did what I always did and knocked gently on it and then went in.

I pushed open the door and froze, stunned at the scene in front of me. At first I thought I must be seeing things, my brain unable to comprehend what I was looking at.

Leo was dressed in a T-shirt and boxer shorts and was sitting on his bed. In his right hand was a compass that he was using to cut the skin on the top of his right thigh over and over. But the thing that struck me the most was the blood.

There seemed to be bright red blood everywhere: oozing out of the top of his left thigh, soaking into his boxer shorts and the duvet beneath him.

'Oh my God, Leo!' I gasped. 'What on earth are you doing? Please stop that now!'

'I did it too deep,' he panicked, blood all over his hands, his eyes wide. 'I'm sorry, Maggie, I didn't mean to do it so deep.'

My heart thumped. My head spun.

There was so much blood.

I was in shock but I could see that Leo was too. His whole body was trembling.

Pull yourself together, I told myself. Stay calm.

I knew I needed to get that compass off him before he could do any more damage to himself.

'Leo, sweetie, give me the compass please,' I told him gently.

He looked up at me, his eyes wide with fear.

'Leo, pass me the compass,' I repeated firmly, holding my hand out to him.

His eyes were glazed and it was as if he was in a trance as he passed it over to me with trembling hands.

'It's all my fault,' he whimpered. 'I let the social workers in.'

Poor, poor boy. The events of today had clearly been going round and round in his mind, tormenting him.

'Leo, you need to listen to me. None of this is your fault,' I told him firmly.

I knew the next thing I urgently needed to do was to try and stop the bleeding. He'd cut himself several times and one of them looked pretty deep. There was a towel drying on the radiator so I grabbed it and pressed it down on his thigh. Leo winced in pain.

'Lovey, I need you to hold this down on your leg for a minute while I run downstairs and get the first-aid kit,' I told him.

Leo nodded. He looked terrified, but thankfully he was compliant.

As I dashed downstairs to the kitchen, so many things were running through my mind. I knew Leo was anxious and upset, but I'd never in a million years suspected that he was hurting himself. Judging by the criss-cross of faded scars that I'd noticed on both his thighs, it was clear this was something that had been going on for a while. I remembered the blood stain I'd found on his school shirt a few weeks ago and his reluctance to go into the swimming pool or have his medical and suddenly it all clicked into place. He hadn't wanted anyone to see his body and realise what he'd been doing to himself.

It was shocking and I felt terrible. Leo must be in so much emotional pain if he was prepared to hurt himself like that. But there was no time to think about it right now.

I ran back upstairs with the first-aid kit. Leo winced as I dabbed his wounds with a medicated wipe, trying to assess how deep the cut was under all the blood.

'Good lad,' I told him. 'Take some nice deep breaths.'

As gently as I could, I taped a dressing across his leg to try to soak up the blood, but the red quickly seeped through.

'I think we need to go to hospital and get this checked out, sweetie,' I told him as calmly as I could.

'No, no way,' he stammered, shaking his head. 'I don't want to go to hospital.'

'We have to, I'm afraid,' I told him firmly. 'One of your cuts is quite deep and you might need some stitches.'

He still didn't seem very happy about it.

'You stay here and I'll go and get you a drink of water,' I told him.

I ran back downstairs to the kitchen. Before I got Leo a drink, I grabbed my phone and called Vicky.

'I'm sorry to call so late but I've got a bit of situation with Leo here and I think I need to take him to hospital.'

'Oh no, Maggie, that's awful,' she sighed. 'I know you can't tell me much, but is it serious?'

'I don't know,' I told her. 'There's a fair bit of blood and I think he needs stitches. Do you mind coming round and waiting here, just in case the girls wake up?'

'Of course not,' she said. 'I'll head over now.'

I took the water back upstairs to Leo. He was sitting on the bed where I'd left him, the dressing on his thigh was now covered in a bloom of red where the blood had soaked through.

'Vicky's coming round to babysit the girls while we go to hospital,' I told him.

'Did you tell her?' he asked anxiously. 'Did you tell her what I'd done?'

I shook my head.

'She knows we need to go to the hospital but I didn't say why,' I reassured him. 'She's a foster carer too, so she understands.'

I helped him to gently pull on a pair of tracksuit bottoms over the bandage and he put on some trainers. We were waiting in the hall by the time Vicky arrived. Leo hung his head in shame and wouldn't look at her as we walked out of the front door.

'Thank you so much,' I said to her.

'I hope you get seen quickly.' She smiled sympathetically.

Leo was silent on the fifteen-minute drive to the local hospital and I didn't push him to speak. I could see he was shaken and he was clearly in shock.

When we got to A&E, we went to the desk to register and then took a seat. I got Leo settled, then I walked off to one side to give my agency a ring. I spoke to the out-of-hours social worker and quickly explained what had happened.

'I'll write up a report tonight and email it to you so you'll have it in the morning, but if they want to keep him in overnight, I'll call you back,' I told her.

'Thanks for letting us know, Maggie,' the worker told me.

'I hope Leo's OK. We'll let the out-of-hours team at Social Services know and also email his social worker.'

When I hung up, I went back to sit with Leo. Thankfully he seemed a bit calmer.

'Are you feeling all right, lovey?' I asked him and he nodded.

'Is this something that you've done before?'

He shrugged his shoulders.

'Did you used to do it at Mum's house too?'

Leo looked down at the floor and nodded.

'I just felt really, really sad and it's the only thing that makes me feel better,' he whispered, looking close to tears. 'I'm a bad person and I know that's why she doesn't want me back.'

'Leo, look at me,' I said to him firmly.

Begrudgingly he looked up at me, his dark eyes shining with tears.

'You are not a bad person, Leo,' I told him. 'Your mum's got a lot of problems and she wants everyone else to take responsibility for them.

'You are not to blame,' I continued. 'It's an adult's job to look after their children and your mum didn't look after you or your sisters. You've done such a good job looking after Amelie and Lexie, but that should never have been your responsibility.'

I desperately wanted him to believe me but I wasn't sure that he did.

A few minutes later a nurse called Leo's name and she led us into a cubicle. She gently took the dressing off and examined his thigh.

'Can you tell me what happened?' she asked him.

He looked down at the bed and refused to speak.

The nurse glanced up at me, her eyebrows raised.

'Leo, do you want me to talk to the nurse for you?' I asked him. 'You can stop me at any time if what I'm saying isn't right.'

He nodded gratefully.

'I found him in his bedroom this evening cutting his thigh with a compass,' I explained. 'Leo has told me that it isn't the first time that this has happened.'

'Oh, pet, why on earth did you do that to yourself?' she sighed.

Leo's head was hung in shame and I could see silent tears streaming down his face.

'It's OK, flower,' I told him, putting my arm around his shoulders. 'It's going to be OK. The doctors and nurses need to know how you did this so they know how to treat you.'

Gently the nurse cleaned up Leo's wounds. It gave me a chance to have a proper look at his thighs. Both of them were covered in scars. Some had healed to a white, some were pink while others were a lot more recent and were red and lumpy. I could see from looking at them that this was definitely something that he'd been doing for a while. This had clearly been the outlet for all his pain and anguish, hidden away under his clothes.

'One of these cuts is quite deep so it's going to need a few stitches,' the nurse said to Leo. 'And you'll need a tetanus jab just in case there's any infection from the compass.'

Then she turned to me.

'Because of how the injury happened, we can't discharge him until he's been assessed by someone from the children's mental health team,' she told me. 'They need to be convinced that it's safe for him to leave.'

'I will be safe,' Leo told her, looking panicked. 'I won't do anything, I promise. I just want to go back and go to bed.'

'We need to make sure, darling,' she told him.

We waited in the same cubical. Leo was very brave as the nurse gave him an injection and stitched up his wound. I was prepared for a long wait but thankfully it was only forty-five minutes before a doctor from the mental health team came down. She was a blonde-haired woman in her forties who was very brusque and businesslike. Leo looked terrified as she marched into the cubical.

'Is it OK to talk in front of your foster carer, or do you want her to leave the room?' she asked him.

'No, I want her to stay,' he said.

The doctor asked him a lot of questions about how he was feeling and why he'd hurt himself. Leo just looked terrified as she reeled them off the list on her clipboard. He clammed up and stared at the floor, refusing to say a word.

'Leo, is it OK if I talk to the doctor on your behalf?' I asked him.

He nodded and I could see the relief on his face that he didn't have to.

'The last few weeks have been very, very difficult for Leo,' I explained. 'He's come into the care system and his biological mother has just decided that she can no longer care for Leo or his sisters. Leo was told the news today so obviously it's been hugely upsetting for him.'

'Are you happy taking him home?' the doctor asked me. 'Do you feel like you can manage the risk?'

'Absolutely.'

'Good.' She smiled. 'I'll make a referral to CAMHS and I'll let Social Services know that I've seen him.'

CAMHS stands for the children and adolescent mental health service.

As Leo and I walked out of the hospital to the car, I could see he was exhausted. It was after midnight by the time we crept in the door, and Vicky, bless her, was asleep on the sofa.

'Let's get you to bed, lovey,' I whispered to Leo, ushering him upstairs. I'd wake Vicky up afterwards.

He quickly got into his pyjamas and brushed his teeth while I checked on the girls. I was relieved to see that they were both still fast asleep. Then I went in to say goodnight to Leo. He still looked so unbelievably sad and it was gut-wrenching.

'Are you feeling any better?' I asked him.

He shrugged.

'You try and get some sleep, flower, and then we'll talk about it tomorrow,' I told him.

He nodded, settling down under the covers.

I went back downstairs and gently shook Vicky awake.

'Sorry, Maggie, I must have nodded off. How's Leo?' she asked, rubbing her eyes.

'He's OK,' I told her. 'He's had a few stitches.'

I explained what had happened and how I'd discovered him self-harming.

'Oh my gosh, that poor lad,' she sighed.

I was thankful that his leg would heal and his scars would fade in time. More worrying were his mental scars.

'I just didn't see it,' I sighed. 'I should have known.'

'Of course you didn't see it,' replied Vicky. 'He was hiding what he was doing under his clothes. He's thirteen, Maggie, it's hardly as if he's a toddler and you were giving him a bath every day. You weren't to know. No wonder he was reluctant to go swimming or have the LAC medical.'

The eating issues were one thing, but it was a genuine shock to discover that he'd been cutting himself too. I knew it was all connected to his sense of self-esteem and self-worth, and for Leo these were at rock bottom.

Vicky gave me a hug.

'I'm off home to my bed now,' she told me. 'Sleep well and things will look better in the morning.'

'I hope so,' I sighed. 'It's felt like the longest day.'

As I locked the door behind Vicky, I felt exhausted, but I knew I couldn't go to bed until I'd typed out my incident report and emailed it to my agency. My eyes felt heavy as I tapped away on my computer. Even as I read back through what I'd written, I still couldn't quite believe what Leo had done.

I'd fostered children in the past who had self-harmed and I'd had training on how to deal with it. But none of that made it any easier to see or experience. I knew a child must be hurting very badly to want to do that to themselves. I knew there were varying degrees of self-harm, from children who bit and tore at the skin around their nails or chewed the inside of their cheeks to those who resorted to cutting or burning themselves.

That night as I lay in bed, shattered but struggling to sleep, I was just relieved that I'd found Leo when I did. I shuddered to think of how much more damage he might have done to himself if I'd left him alone much longer.

★

The next morning, I woke up early and went downstairs. I wanted to put anything sharp in the kitchen out of the way just in case. I took the kitchen scissors and carving knives from the drawer and put them in a high cupboard, and I collected all the nail scissors and eyebrow tweezers from the bathroom cabinet. Just after 7 a.m., Leo came downstairs. I was surprised to see he was wearing his school uniform.

'How are you feeling, lovey?' I asked him. 'You had a late night so I thought you might want to stay at home today.'

'No, I'm fine and my leg feels OK,' he said firmly. 'I want to go to school.'

'OK,' I told him. 'But if you're going to go into school, I have to let them know what happened last night.'

He shook his head. 'Why do you have to tell them?' he asked, looking furious. 'Why do you have to tell anyone? I'm not going to do anything at school.'

'Because it's both my job and the school's job to keep you safe,' I explained. 'They need to be aware of this so they can help you if you need it. It doesn't mean anyone's going to do anything or say anything to you.'

Leo grudgingly nodded, but he didn't look happy about it.

'I'm also going to have to tell Alex, sweetie, because that's part of my job too,' I added.

'You're not going to tell my sisters, are you?' he asked, looking worried.

'No, of course not,' I replied. 'They're only little and I don't want to scare them.'

I insisted on dropping him off at school that morning before we took Amelie. After everything that had happened the day before, I wanted to make sure that he was OK.

'Why are we taking Leo to school?' asked Amelie as we got into the car.

'Ooh, it's a special treat just because we're all ready in time today and it saves Leo getting the bus.' I smiled.

When I got home, I left Lexie to play with some Duplo while I rang Leo's form tutor Mrs Collins. I explained what had happened last night and that I'd taken Leo to hospital.

'We'll keep an eye on him and make sure there's someone available to talk to if he needs it.'

'Thank you. I don't think it's an issue in school but I thought you should know.'

As soon as I put down the phone down, Alex rang.

'Oh, Maggie, I heard what happened last night,' she sighed. 'How is Leo doing?'

'It completely took me by surprise but judging by all the marks on his legs it's something that he's been doing for a long time,' I sighed.

'Poor boy, he's obviously a lot more troubled than we thought,' replied Alex. 'Do you think he meant to hurt himself?'

'I think it's his outlet for his fear and his anger and upset, but I don't think he's suicidal,' I told her. 'I think he cut a lot deeper than he meant to and he scared himself.'

'Maybe having to go to hospital will put him off doing it again?' suggested Alex.

Sadly, I knew it was unlikely to be as simple as that.

'I'll come round and talk to him myself, but in the meantime have you done a risk assessment at home?' she asked.

'Don't worry, I already did that this morning,' I explained, and told her how I'd hidden away anything sharp.

When Leo came home from school that afternoon, I asked him to leave his rucksack downstairs.

'While you're feeling like this, I don't want you to have anything sharp in your room. Are you going to be able to manage that or do you need me to check your room for you?' I asked him.

'I'll manage it,' he told me, looking sheepish. 'I'm sorry, Maggie.'

'You don't have to be sorry,' I replied. 'I just want to keep you safe.'

But to be honest, I knew if Leo wanted to harm himself, he could use anything from a paperclip to a fork. I couldn't hide everything from him. There had to be a certain element of trust. I also explained that if he was going to be in his room for long periods of time, I wanted him to always leave the door open except when he was going to sleep.

No matter what measures I put in place, I knew I was going to spend the next few days on tenterhooks, wondering what Leo was up to and whether he was going to hurt himself again. It was stressful, but at least I knew now. All I could hope was that there was an element of relief for Leo that his secret was finally out in the open and that he would accept my help.

TEN

Keeping Safe

My past experiences of fostering children who self-harm had been that some of them were very happy to talk about it while others were incredibly secretive. Some would confide in me when they wanted to cut themselves while others closed down and didn't want to talk at all. In the days after I'd discovered Leo was hurting himself, it was clear that he was very much in the latter camp.

I knew enough about self-harm to know that it was both addictive and a way of letting off steam, releasing some of the internal pain into something physical. I still felt that Leo wasn't suicidal; clearly cutting himself was his way of coping with his emotional pain. Like his issues around eating, hurting himself gave him some element of control in his chaotic life. It was his outlet for all the grief, anger and rejection that he felt and perhaps couldn't verbalise. I wanted to try and make Leo see that he didn't have to hurt himself, and help him to put some coping strategies in place. I also knew how stretched CAMHS were, and even if Alex flagged him up as a priority, there were sadly so many children in crisis it could be months before he got an appointment with a therapist.

As much as I tried to act normally over the next few days, I found that I was constantly on high alert. I was always trying to sense Leo's mood in case he was thinking about hurting himself again.

A couple of days after I'd taken him to hospital, Leo came in from school and disappeared straight off upstairs to his room.

'Leo, where are you going?' I called after him, trying to keep my voice neutral.

'Just to my room to read a book,' he yelled.

I followed him up the stairs so the girls wouldn't hear what I was saying.

'Are you OK to be up there by yourself?' I asked him.

It was a subtle way of me asking if he was about to hurt himself. However, Leo looked puzzled and I could tell that he didn't understand what I was getting at.

'I mean, are you safe being on your own at the moment, in that you're not going to go upstairs and do anything to hurt yourself?' I asked him.

'Why are you even saying that?' he snapped. 'I'm just going to read my book.'

'I'm sorry, lovey,' I told him. 'But after what happened the other night, whenever you go upstairs to your room, I'm always going to worry whether you're OK. I'm afraid you're going to have to put up with me asking you.'

Leo looked both embarrassed and annoyed.

'Why are you even bothered?' he sighed. 'My mum wasn't. She never even noticed I was doing it.'

'Well I have noticed, Leo, and I care about you,' I told him. 'I know you're hurting and I want to help you. You don't have to do this on your own, lovey. If you talk to me about it, then we can try and find some ways to help you.'

'I don't want to talk and I don't want help,' he spat.

He stomped up the stairs and slammed his bedroom door. I felt sick with worry about what was going on behind that closed door. The thought of him hurting himself and ending up in hospital again was too much to bear.

You have to trust him, I told myself.

It took all my strength to stay downstairs and play with Lexie and Amelie without going up to check on him. I lasted half an hour before it got too much and I went upstairs. As if to prove a point to me, Leo had opened his bedroom door and I could see that he was lying on his bed reading.

'See,' he hissed. 'I told you I was reading. Is that allowed?'

'Of course it's allowed.' I smiled, my stomach sinking with relief.

I sat down on the end of his bed.

'Leo, I've looked after children in the past who have hurt themselves like you do and I've found it often helps them to have some kind of distraction,' I told him.

He looked at me wide-eyed with surprise.

'What, you know other people who do this?' he asked, looking amazed.

'Sadly, yes.' I nodded. 'I know it's horrible when you're feeling that way, but what made it easier for them to cope or stop altogether was having something else to distract them,' I replied. 'So the next time you feel like you might want to hurt yourself, come and find me. It doesn't matter what else

I'm doing, even if I'm asleep, just come and wake me up and we can find a distraction together.'

Leo looked deep in thought.

'What kind of thing is a distraction?' he asked curiously.

'I know it sounds a bit silly, but some people find that playing with Play-Doh helps them.'

Leo rolled his eyes.

'Play-Doh?' he laughed. 'That's what little kids like Lexie have.'

'I told you it might sound silly, but it's actually a really good distraction,' I told him. 'It keeps your hands busy and you can knead it and stretch it and squish it and take all your anger out on it.'

'I'm thirteen, I'm not into Play-Doh,' he sighed.

'Well, there are other things you can try too,' I told him.

I talked him through some of the other things that I'd tried over the years with self-harmers, such as giving them a glass of ice cubes to crunch in their mouths or wrapping some ice cubes in a towel and holding it on the area where they would usually hurt themselves. The idea was that it would give them a temporary feeling of the discomfort that usually came from cutting themselves. An even simpler idea was to hold an ice cube in their hand until it melted.

'I know you probably think I'm mad suggesting all these strange things,' I told him, smiling.

Leo grinned shyly and nodded.

'And you might find that none of them work for you,' I continued. 'But you don't know until you try, and it might help you feel a little more in control of things.

'I know that it's hard for you to talk about it sometimes, but if you're feeling like you want to hurt yourself, then you can just come down and say you want some ice. That can be our code,' I told him. 'I'm not going to get angry or upset. I just want to help you, OK?'

He nodded.

'OK,' he sighed.

All I could do was hope that he meant it and I kept my fingers crossed that he would ask me for help when the time came.

While I was constantly watching Leo like a hawk, worrying if he was OK, I also had to be there for the girls. While their brother's mental health was a continuing cause for concern, they were flourishing. Amelie was enjoying school and her reading was really coming on. She now insisted on reading pages from their bedtime story herself, and Lexie was getting into arts and crafts. While Leo and Amelie were at school, we were painting, sticking, gluing and stencilling. She was very creative and for a three-year-old she had great concentration.

A few days later, I'd just put the girls to bed and was about to sit down in front of *Coronation Street* when Leo wandered into the living room.

'Come and sit down with me, lovey,' I told him. 'We can watch something else if you like. Do you fancy a film?'

He shook his head, looking on edge, and started wandering around the living room.

'Please come and sit with me, Leo,' I repeated. 'You're making me nervous pacing up and down like that. Do you want to play cards or a board game?'

'No, I don't want to,' he said.

There was something about the way he was acting that rang alarm bells. It was like he was on the edge of saying something to me but he couldn't quite get the words out.

'Are you feeling that you might want to cut yourself, flower?' I asked him.

I could see by the horrified look on his face that he was taken aback at how direct and matter-of-fact I was being about it.

'No!' he snapped, looking shocked.

'OK, I thought I'd ask, just in case,' I said.

Rather than asking any more questions, I decided to go into the kitchen and make a cup of tea to give him a bit of breathing space.

When I came back into the living room a few minutes later, Leo was still pacing up and down.

'Maggie, you were right,' he said quietly, not looking at me. 'I think I might need some ice.'

'OK,' I said calmly. 'Let's see what we can do about that then.'

I wanted to show Leo that if he was open and honest with me about wanting to self-harm, I wouldn't get upset or angry with him. It was hard for me not to panic, but I made sure not to change my tone of voice and tried to remain normal and measured, even though inside I wasn't feeling calm at all.

I took Leo into the kitchen and he watched me, intrigued, as I got some ice out of the freezer and wrapped it in a hand towel.

'Let's try this,' I told him gently. 'Roll up your pyjama leg and press this on your thigh and see how it feels.'

He hesitated and looked a bit unsure.

'Give it a try.' I smiled. 'If it hurts your cut, then try the other leg.'

114

'No, it will be OK,' he replied.

I went over to the sink while he put the towel on the criss-cross of scars on his thigh.

'Gosh, that's really cold,' he gasped.

'Leo, they're ice cubes – they're going to be cold!' I teased. 'If it gets too much, you can take it off.'

He left it a little while, then took it off and rubbed his leg.

'Try the other side if you want,' I told him.

He put it on his other thigh and winced, although he left it there for a few minutes.

'Brrr, watching you with those ice cubes has made me really cold now.' I shivered after a few minutes. 'I think I'm going to make myself a hot chocolate. Would you like one?'

Leo nodded.

I walked over to the kettle. I wasn't sure how successful that had been, but at least it had distracted him and I was relieved to see that he didn't seem quite so agitated now.

'Shall I put the ice cubes back in the freezer?' he asked me.

'No, flower, just put them in the sink,' I replied. 'Pour some hot water on them if you want.'

While I made us a drink, Leo stared at the ice cubes as they crackled and melted in the sink. Then we sat at the kitchen table and had our hot chocolates.

'How are you feeling?' I said, keeping my voice light.

'I know what you're asking,' he sighed, rolling his eyes. 'But don't worry, I don't feel like that any more.'

'Good,' I replied.

I didn't go on about it, I just left it there.

'Do you want to watch some telly with me?' I suggested.

Leo shook his head.

'I'm really tired, I think I'll just go to bed,' he said.

I couldn't tell whether the ice had worked or had been a complete waste of time, but I just hoped he meant it, and wasn't going to go upstairs and hurt himself.

As the days passed, I started to realise that the vulnerable time for Leo, when he felt most sad, angry or unhappy, was at night. He was often tired after his day at school and in the evening had more time alone with his thoughts. Other times, I would find that something like a social worker visit had triggered it .

It was another evening, about a week later, when he came downstairs and asked for ice cubes. When I checked in the freezer, I realised we didn't have any more left.

Leo looked panicked and I wracked my brains as to what to do. I knew I had to come up with something else quickly.

'Actually, I'm glad there's no ice cubes because I know another thing you can try that might make you feel better,' I told him, an idea suddenly popping into my head.

It was a technique that another foster carer had told me about years ago, and I'd tried it with a fifteen-year-old girl who was self-harming. The idea is to give the child a red felt-tip pen and let them draw the lines on their skin where they would usually cut themselves. The red pen gave the idea of seeing blood without the person actually having to harm themselves. I knew Leo might think it was ridiculous, but I thought it was at least worth a try. I rummaged around in the cupboard until I found the tub of colouring pens.

'Roll your pyjama legs up,' I told him.

Leo raised his eyebrows at me, looking uncertain, but he did as I asked. Then I handed him the red pen.

'I want you to pretend the pen is a compass and slash your leg.'

He looked at me like I'd gone mad.

'What, you want me to draw on my own leg?' he asked, looking perplexed.

I nodded. 'Press as hard as you want,' I told him. 'And after you've drawn a line on your leg, I want you to write down a word on this piece of paper. It can be any word at all. Anything that describes how you're feeling.'

Up until now, Leo had seemed intrigued when I'd talked to him about alternatives to hurting himself. I had sensed that, as anxious and on edge as he was, he was desperate to find an alternative way of channelling his emotions. But this time, he looked at the pen for a moment before throwing it down on the table.

'This is so stupid,' he cried. 'That's obviously not going to work. I don't want to draw on my legs or write stupid things. It's not going to help.'

'Please just give it a go,' I urged him. 'Indulge me and my stupid ideas. I don't mind if you only write down one word or just scribble on the paper. It doesn't matter.'

He looked down and did one half-hearted streak on his thigh.

'Try it again and press down as hard as you want,' I urged him.

He slashed at his thigh, the pen clutched tightly in his fist. He glanced up at me, uncertain, and I nodded at him encouragingly. It was like seeing the floodgates open, and Leo repeated the motion furiously, again and again, until his thigh was covered in red pen marks. I shuddered to think of him actually hurting himself like that.

'Now write down how you feel,' I told him, when he'd finished.

He frantically scribbled down a few words on a piece of paper. I didn't look at them or ask him what they were.

'If you want you can save them and we can talk about them another time,' I said gently. 'Or you can keep them private, it's up to you.'

He looked down at his thighs that were covered in red pen, and it was almost as though he was coming back to reality.

'My legs look ridiculous,' he sighed, sounding exhausted all of a sudden.

'I'll go and get some baby wipes – that should get it off,' I told him. 'It's a good job I didn't give you a permanent marker.'

Leo gave me a weak smile.

I wasn't sure if this new exercise had helped, or whether he just thought I was mad, but at least the crisis seemed to be over. I was relieved that Leo seemed calmer now.

As I went to get the baby wipes, I saw him scrunch up the piece of paper and stuff it into his dressing-gown pocket. I didn't say any more about it, and simply brought him the wipes for him to clean up with. Leo seemed subdued, but the anxiety and tension thankfully seemed to have eased, and I felt relieved as I walked him upstairs and he wished me goodnight.

I suspected that he'd kept the piece of paper though, and a few days later I decided to ask him. He was reading in bed and I popped in to say goodnight.

'Remember those words that you wrote down the other night?' I asked him, sitting on the edge of his bed. 'I just wondered if you had kept hold of them?'

Leo's cheeks went red.

'I don't want to talk about it,' he snapped. 'They're private.'

'No problem,' I replied. 'I just thought that it might help if we talked about them.'

He sighed and reluctantly took the crumpled piece of paper out of his bedside table.

'OK, fine,' he snapped. 'If it gets you off my back.'

Leo threw the ball of scrunched-up paper at me and then rolled over and faced the wall. I unravelled it. There, written in capital letters in red pen were three words.

Scared. Bad. Angry.

As I read them, a lump formed in my throat.

It was gut-wrenching to see the raw emotions Leo was feeling right there in front of me.

'What's making you scared, Leo?' I asked him gently.

'I just don't know what's going to happen to me and my sisters,' he mumbled, his face still firmly turned to the wall.

'I know, sweetie, and I can imagine that is really scary. But what's happening at the moment is that you're all staying here with me. I promise that any time I know anything new, or Alex tells me something, the first thing that we will do is make sure we pass that information on to you,' I told him.

'I know it's hard, but you just have to trust us, flower. It's going to be OK.'

I looked back down at the other words.

'Why do you think you're bad, Leo?'

'Cos it's my fault Social Services took us off Mum.'

'That's not your fault, Leo,' I told him. 'The school rang Social Services, not you. They did that because they needed to keep you and your sisters safe. But you had nothing to do with Social Services making the decision to take you away from your mum. That wasn't your fault at all, Leo. You had nothing to do with it, OK?'

He nodded sadly, but the look on his face made it clear that he was still shouldering the blame for everything that had happened to him and his sisters. I knew it was going to take him a long time to stop believing that.

'Who are you angry with?' I asked gently.

'My mum,' he sighed. 'I just don't understand why she doesn't care about me or Lexie or Amelie.'

'Some people show that they care in strange ways,' I explained. 'What your mum has done might actually be the best care that she can give you at the moment. By doing this, she knows that other people are looking after you and your sisters properly when she couldn't.'

Leo didn't say anything and he still wouldn't turn around to look at me.

'These are your words, Leo, and you can look at them any time you need to,' I told him. 'Or any time that you feel like it, we can write down new words together if you want and we can talk them through.'

Even though he was still turned away from me, I saw him nod.

'I know this is all so hard for you, and I'm so proud of you for trying,' I told him. He didn't say anything, but I hoped something in my words would sink in.

It was impossible to tell whether any of this was going to help Leo stop self-harming in the long term. It was certainly never going to be something that disappeared overnight because it had been brought on by long-term damage; Leo's way of dealing with years of hurt and pain. All I could do was try to support him as best I could, and hope that somehow, something would help him feel less alone so that eventually he could stop putting himself through this hell.

A few weeks later, after a fair bit of pressure from Alex, Leo got an appointment with a therapist at CAMHS. Vicky had agreed to look after Lexie for a few hours so I could take him and he had the afternoon off school.

As we pulled up outside the modern glass building where our local CAMHS was based, I could see Leo was nervous.

'What will I have to do?' he asked anxiously. 'What are they going to ask me?'

'You don't need to worry, lovey,' I reassured him. 'And you don't have to talk about anything you don't want to. It's just a good chance for you to talk, and for the person you're talking with to help you work out your feelings.'

'How are they gonna do that?' he scoffed.

I used the example that I had used with a lot of children in the past when they were starting therapy.

'Imagine that you're carrying around a big bag filled to the brim with all sorts of worries and stresses, and every time you open this bag, all these things just came spilling out. There's no order to them and you feel completely overwhelmed and unable to carry the bag around any more because it's so heavy.

'What a therapist will help you do is pull out a worry, look at that worry and work out what you can do with it. When you've sorted out a worry, you don't need to put it back in the bag, so you can get rid of it. It means your bag isn't as heavy any more, and things don't just keep spilling out all the time.'

'That's stupid,' Leo sighed, rolling his eyes. 'I don't even have a big bag, I've got a rucksack.'

'It's just a way of thinking about things, Leo,' I told him gently. 'Hopefully the therapist will help you clear a bit of space in your head and make things feel lighter for you. Surely that's worth a try, isn't it?'

He shrugged and didn't look very convinced. Many children were reluctant to see a therapist, but then found that they actually enjoyed the sessions. I had always found that the therapy helped them in the long run.

After half an hour in the waiting room, Leo and I were taken through to a therapy room. It was a bit like the contact rooms, with comfy chairs and sofas and toys and books for younger children. Leo looked increasingly uneasy.

Two female therapists introduced themselves. Sarah and Di were both in their late thirties or early forties and were dressed casually in jeans and sweatshirts. It was clear that they tried to make everything feel as relaxed as possible to put the children at ease, but Leo looked on edge.

'Maggie, do you want to come with me?' Sarah asked me, after a minute or two of small talk.

Leo looked like he was about to jump up and come with me.

'You'll be fine,' I reassured him. 'I'm only going into the other room.'

It was deliberately set up like this so that Leo had the security of me coming into the room with him, and then, rather than him having to go off with a stranger into a different room, he could remain there and talk with Di. Then, at the end of the session, I would go back into the room to rejoin him.

Sarah took me into her office and we went through some basic information about Leo: his date of birth, when he had come into the care system, his family set-up, what I'd noticed about him in the time he'd been with me. As I answered Sarah's questions, I couldn't stop my mind from ticking in the background, wondering how Leo was getting on in the other room.

Half an hour later we went back in to join Leo and Di. Leo was slouched in the chair, his arms crossed and scowling as we walked in. It was clear from the atmosphere in the room that it hadn't gone well.

'Leo, Maggie and I had a good chat about when you came into the care system and a bit about your family background,' Sarah told him, keeping her voice light.

Leo didn't say anything, but just picked at the hem of his jumper, looking furious.

'Unfortunately, Leo didn't feel able to talk to me today, but that's absolutely fine because we're still getting to know each other.' Di smiled.

'That's OK, Leo,' Sarah told him gently. 'There's always next time and now you know what to expect, hopefully it won't be as daunting.'

He remained silent, then grabbed his coat and bag, and I smiled apologetically at the two women.

I knew Leo well enough by now to tell that he was het up and angry, so I waited until we got into the car to talk to him.

'So how did that go?' I asked him tentatively as I put on my seatbelt.

'I don't ever want to go back there,' he spat.

'Why's that?' I asked him. 'Di seemed very nice.'

'Talking to you is bad enough. I don't want to talk to other people too. I don't want them asking me loads of questions.'

'I promise you it will feel better next week, lovey,' I told him. 'Next time you'll know what to expect.'

But Leo refused to say any more. I could see he had shut himself down so I decided not to push him.

'I'm going up to my room,' he muttered as soon as we got home.

'Leo, are you safe?' I asked him gently.

'Yes!' he snapped. 'Why do you keep asking me that stupid question all the time?'

'Because it's my job to keep you safe and I need to know that you are,' I told him.

He didn't reply, stomped upstairs and I heard his bedroom door slam. I went into the living room where Vicky was playing with Lexie.

'That's doesn't sound good,' she sighed, giving me a sympathetic look.

'I think the therapy was a bit much for him,' I said.

I went and sat down with them, but my mind was on Leo upstairs. I knew that being this upset and agitated would be a prime trigger for his self-harm.

'I'm just going to nip upstairs and check on him,' I told her.

As I knocked on his bedroom door and pushed it open, I feared the worst and steeled myself for what I might be about to walk in on.

But to my surprise, Leo was curled up on his bed sobbing.

'Oh, lovey,' I sighed, sitting down beside him. 'It's OK.'

He sat up and his face was puffy and swollen. He hurriedly tried to dry his eyes, and he looked mortified that I'd found him crying.

'I just didn't like her talking to me,' he sobbed. 'I don't know her and she doesn't know anything. She's not going to be able to help. No one can make me feel better.'

'Oh, flower,' I sighed. 'I know it must be so hard.'

I put my arms around him and he sank into me and cried.

My heart felt heavy for him. Could I help him to stop self-harming or was it all becoming too much? Would he ever be able to move on from his past and stop blaming himself for everything that had happened?

ELEVEN

A Bombshell

'It's so good to see you.' I grinned at Louisa as I flicked the kettle on and got out a plate of Hobnobs.

She had a day off from work so she'd popped round for a coffee.

'How's Charlie?' I asked her. 'And the flat?'

'Charlie's fine.' She smiled. 'Working hard as usual and the flat is great. I love buying bits and bobs for it.'

Although it had been several months since she'd moved out, I still really missed having Louisa around and I relished our time together.

As I poured the tea, Lexie came skipping over to Louisa and shyly asked her if she'd paint her nails for her again.

'Oh yes, I'm very good at manicures.' Louisa nodded. 'Let me have my cup of tea and chat to Maggie and then I promise I'll do your nails, OK?'

Lexie nodded and scampered off to play.

'I love those blonde curls,' sighed Louisa. 'She's such a cutie.'

'She really is,' I agreed.

'How are the girls getting on?' she asked.

'Really well, to be honest.' I shrugged. 'I'd expected them to be very unsettled after everything that's happened to them recently, but they're both very resilient.'

Amelie seemed to be happy at school, and the following week Lexie was due to start going to the local nursery in the mornings for three hours. I wasn't sure how she was going to settle in but, so far, she seemed excited about it.

'Do you know yet what's going to happen to the children long term?' Louisa asked. 'Are you keeping them?'

'To be honest, I've got no idea,' I told her. 'I've been so caught up with Leo and his problems that I haven't had time to think about anything else.'

The last I'd heard from Alex, Social Services were going to go to court for a full care order. All my time and energy had been so focused on Leo and how I could help him that I hadn't really thought about future plans.

A couple of days later, I went to a parent–teacher meeting at Amelie's school.

'She's doing so well.' Miss Hughes smiled when I went into the classroom to see her. 'I'm amazed at the change in her. She's a lot more confident, she's making friends and her reading and writing are really coming on.'

Miss Hughes explained that she had been doing one-to-one reading with Amelie the other day and part of the story was about a mother who had gone on holiday without her children.

'Amelie said that her mummy had gone too and she wasn't going to see her any more,' she told me, looking worried. 'Is that true, Maggie?'

'I'm afraid so,' I replied. 'Their mum has decided not to fight for custody, so Amelie and her siblings are going to be staying in care.'

'Oh no,' sighed Miss Hughes. 'That's really sad.'

'It is,' I agreed. 'But sometimes it's for the best in the long run.'

Sad as it was, it was good to know that Amelie had understood what Alex and I had told her.

Indeed, Amelie and Lexie seemed to be thriving. Miss Hughes had told me Amelie's closest friend was a little girl called Tilly, so I suggested to Amelie that we invite her round to play after school. Amelie was ecstatic and she couldn't wait to show Tilly her bedroom and her favourite toys.

'I've never had a friend come to my house before,' she whispered to me with a massive grin on her face.

It was so lovely to see her excitement.

'Can I get a friend too?' asked Lexie, clearly feeling left out.

'Well I'm sure you'll make lots of friends when you start nursery next week and you can invite one of them round for a play.'

Lexie smiled.

Suddenly I was struck by the difference between the girls and their big brother. Amelie and Lexie were flourishing in their new life. I was sure that there would always be an element of sadness about their mum, particularly as they got older and understood the situation better, but as things were, they seemed to be thriving on having a routine and some normality and stability.

Meanwhile poor Leo was still struggling. As far as I knew, he hadn't been self-harming, but after a few months with me, he was still regularly wetting the bed and only eating small amounts. Under Alex's guidance, I was giving him lots of high-fat foods and drinks to try and bulk him up and get calories down him whenever I could, but he was still painfully thin. He was also still refusing to open up in his therapy sessions. I often found myself worrying about how best to reach this troubled boy.

The following week it was Lexie's first day at nursery. I'd got her a place at a lovely local nursery in a nearby village. It was small and friendly and I knew the staff who worked there well. Even though I was convinced that she'd love it, I could see she was still very nervous, and it was understandable. Jade had never taken her to playgroups and even though she was a sociable little thing, she'd never been to nursery.

'Leo, I don't want to go to big school,' she told him that morning, her big blue eyes wide.

He picked her up and sat her on his knee.

'You'll be OK, Lex,' he told her reassuringly. 'I bet there will be loads of cool toys there for you to play with and you can do painting and sticking and gluing. And you might even get a drink and a snack.'

Lexie looked over at me for confirmation.

'Yep.' I nodded, smiling at her and Leo. 'I know they do lovely chopped-up fruit and I've heard that sometimes they even have biscuits as a special treat.'

'Yummy!' yelled Lexie excitedly as she leapt off Leo's knee and jumped around the room.

He knew exactly what to say to reassure his sister and win her over. After we'd done the school run with Amelie, we drove to the nursery. Different nurseries and schools have different settling-in methods. I'd spoken to the nursery staff and they felt, rather staying with her, it would be worth trying to leave Lexie for half an hour for her first session. I agreed – sometimes when there was a long settling-in period and you stayed with a child, it was easy for them to get confused and think you were always going to be there.

As we walked into the church hall, Lexie grabbed my hand nervously and I gave it a reassuring squeeze.

'Oh look, Leo was right.' I smiled, pointing to a table covered in all sorts of craft stuff. 'There's sticking and gluing over there, and it looks like they've got all sorts of exciting pipe cleaners and feathers and sequins.'

Before I could say anything else, Lexie was off like a shot, and quickly settled down to make herself a princess crown with some other little girls.

'She'll be absolutely fine,' one of the key workers reassured me. 'You go.'

When I went over to say goodbye, she hardly even looked up.

Her first session went brilliantly and when I went to pick her up, she was full of chatter about all the things that she'd done. When I dropped her off the following day, she ran over to some other children with hardly a backward glance. After months of sitting at home with her mum, shoved in front of the TV, nursery was like a treasure trove of things to interest her lively mind. She'd slowly weened herself off her reliance on television and had got used to playing with toys at my house – now there was no stopping her. It was so lovely to see this sweet little girl growing and thriving.

One morning the following week, Alex came round to see me when the children were all out at school and nursery. I was surprised to see her. Usually she would ring me for an update unless there was anything significant to discuss.

'Oh, I didn't expect to see you today,' I said to her.

'I was just passing and thought I would pop in.' She smiled.

'How are the children doing?' she asked as we sat down at the kitchen table with a cup of coffee.

'The girls are really finding their feet.' I grinned. 'It's Lexie's first week at nursery and so far she seems fine. She's settled really well and she skips in happily every morning.'

I also told her about the parents evening that I'd gone to at Amelie's school and how well she was doing.

'And how's Leo this week?'

'He's doing OK,' I sighed. 'Thankfully we haven't had any more episodes of self-harm since I took him to hospital, and I'm trying to encourage him to be open and honest about it. He's been coming to me whenever he has the urge to hurt himself, so hopefully he feels a little more able to talk about it now. He's still not eating brilliantly, but I'm trying hard to get extra calories into him with plenty of hot milky drinks and things.'

'And how's his relationship with his sisters?' she asked.

'Oh, they've all still got a really strong bond and are incredibly close,' I told her. 'The girls aren't as fearful of going places or doing things without Leo any more, but they always check where he is and that he's going to be back from school later on.'

Alex nodded. 'Actually, that's what I wanted to talk to you about today,' she said, taking a sip of her coffee.

'As you know, the children have been with you for three months now,' she told me. 'I've been chatting to my manager about what we feel is the best way forward for them.'

'Of course,' I said.

Alex explained they now had a full care order from the courts so their thoughts had turned to the long-term plan.

Then she paused. Suddenly she looked nervous, and I started to feel uneasy about what she was about to tell me.

'We've got the review coming up next week so we can talk about this in more detail then, but I think my manager and I are both in agreement that adoption is probably the best way forward.'

I was shocked.

'Wow, really?' I asked, surprised. 'Do you think you'll be able to find someone who'd be willing to take on three children? I honestly thought that you'd rule out adoption because of Leo's age.'

I knew larger sibling groups were always hard to place, particularly when there was such a big age gap between children.

Alex shifted awkwardly in her seat.

'Maggie, I'm not sure if you're quite getting what I'm saying here,' she said gently. 'We feel that adoption is the way forward . . .'

She paused.

'But for the girls, not for Leo.'

I looked at her, confused. Suddenly the penny dropped and the horrible truth dawned on me.

'Surely you can't mean separating them?' I gasped. 'You want to split them up?'

'Yes, we'd be looking at doing what we call a split adoption.' Alex nodded. 'The girls will hopefully be matched fairly quickly and easily with new adoptive parents, but because of Leo's age and his emotional difficulties, we'd be looking at a long-term foster placement rather than adoption for him.'

I couldn't believe what I was hearing. I felt sick to my stomach.

'Alex, you know these children,' I said to her. 'You've seen them. You know how strong their bond is. This will absolutely destroy them.'

I couldn't even begin to imagine how terrible it would be for Leo if he lost his sisters.

'Maggie, I know it's really hard, but I think it's our only option,' she told me. 'Realistically, it's always hard to place a large sibling group for adoption and I just don't think we're going to find a couple who wants all three of them. Two angelic little girls, yes. But a troubled teenage boy who self-harms and has an eating disorder? You know as well as I do that it's just not going to happen, and given the girls' ages, it would be better to get them placed sooner rather than later.'

As hard as it was to accept, I knew what Alex was saying was true.

'Why just focus on adoption, then?' I asked her. 'What about keeping them in long-term foster care? That way all three of them could stay together. I'd be willing to consider taking them on in the long term if you're worried about finding another carer.'

Alex shook her head.

'Thank you for offering, Maggie, but my manager and I don't think it's fair that we deny the girls the chance of finding their own forever family. They're three and five, they're still so very young. They deserve the chance of having a mummy and a daddy of their own, and staying together.

'The other option is that they languish in the care system in the long term all because of their big brother's problems. I know it might sound harsh, but we have to face facts,' Alex told me firmly. 'The girls are very adoptable, but Leo isn't.'

I could see what she was saying. With their corkscrew blonde curls, big blue eyes and happy chatter, Lexie and Amelie were adorable little girls who would be snapped up by potential adopters, but who would want to take on a sulky thirteen-year-old with a history of eating issues, self-harm, anxiety and depression?

In my head, I knew Alex was right, but my heart was screaming that this wasn't fair. All I could think about was Leo, and the devastating impact this was going to have on him.

'This will destroy the girls too,' I told Alex. 'Leo is their stability. He's been like a parent figure to them their whole lives and they're so reliant on him. They've never had a father, they've lost their mother and now they're facing losing Leo too.'

'Perhaps that's another reason why we need to separate them?' suggested Alex. 'It's not good for all three of them to have that sort of dependency on each other. I think that in time the girls will move on and ultimately be able to move past it.'

As a foster carer, I knew that I could air my views, but ultimately the decision about the children's future would be made by Social Services as they were the ones who had parental responsibility for them. I had often found this situation frustrating during my years as a foster carer. Out of all the people involved in these children's care, I was the one who lived with these children, knew their needs and saw the kind of relationships they had. But my opinion was never going to influence the outcome as I was 'just' the foster carer. Alex seemed pretty convinced about what the way forward needed to be and I knew nothing I could say would change her mind.

I felt sick to my stomach as I thought of the impact this was going to have on Leo. He was already crippled by rejection and anger that his mother had given up on him, and he adored his little sisters.

'If his sisters get a new family and he doesn't, it will destroy him,' I pleaded with Alex. 'I don't know whether he would ever be able to get over that. It could affect him for the rest of his life.'

'Like I said, I know it's going to be hard, but we do feel this is the best way to proceed,' repeated Alex. 'But we'll talk about it more at the review meeting and get everyone else's opinion too.'

When Alex left, my head was spinning and I felt close to tears. Thankfully, I'd never had to oversee a split adoption before, but I knew they were increasingly common. There were conflicting arguments on both sides. I'd read articles on the negative impact of keeping children from dysfunctional families together, but I'd also seen studies that had found sibling relationships were *the* most important relationships for children in care. My own personal view was everything possible should be done to preserve that link and keep siblings together.

I decided to phone my supervising social worker Becky and talk to her about it. She could hear how upset I was as soon as she answered the phone.

'I can't believe they're going to separate them,' I said to her, struggling to keep my voice steady.

'What if it sends Leo spiralling into a depression and he starts self-harming again?' I sighed. 'It's going to be devastating for both him and the girls. How are Lexie and Amelie going to cope without the stability of having their big brother around, after everything they've all been through?'

Becky was a good listener.

'I know what you're saying, Maggie, but I can also see Alex's point about the benefits of adoption for the girls,' she told me.

'I understand that individually it would be better for the girls to be adopted, but they're not individuals – they're part of a family unit and I don't want to be involved in breaking that up,' I pleaded with her. 'Why can't Leo stay with them and they can be fostered?'

'I know, Maggie, but is it really fair to keep two little ones in the care system for the rest of their lives when they could so easily be adopted?' asked Becky. 'Leo's only got another five years in the care system whereas the girls have got another fifteen. Don't they deserve the chance to have a family of their own?'

I understood the arguments, but it didn't mean that I agreed with them. I had lived with these children 24/7 for three months and I knew how close their bond was.

To be honest, I was dreading the review meeting. I knew, no matter what I said, I wouldn't be able to change Social Service's decision if they agreed to separate the children. All I could do was give my opinion. As their foster carer, I was the children's advocate, and Leo was one of those children. I strongly believed that he needed his sisters in his life and that the family unit shouldn't be split.

*

The review meeting was being held at my house while Lexie was at nursery and Amelie and Leo were at school. It would be chaired by the independent reviewing officer (IRO), who had just been appointed. She hadn't met the children, but her role was to make sure Social Services were carrying out their duties and responsibilities towards them. The IRO was a woman called Paula Harry. I hadn't met her before, but Alex introduced us and she seemed very nice. She was very tall and had the longest hair that I'd ever seen. It flowed past her waist and looked as though it was long enough for her to sit on. My supervising social worker Becky was there, along with Miss Hughes, Amelie's teacher, and Leo's form tutor Mrs Collins.

'I've spoken with Alex and her manager and they've told me how the long-term plan is for a split adoption for the girls and long-term foster care for Leo,' Paula began, once everyone was settled.

'So what I want to do today is look at how we think the girls would manage with adoption and how Leo would cope being separated from his sisters. It's also a chance for us to talk through how the children are getting on generally.'

Alex quickly outlined when and how the children had been taken into care and how their mother had relinquished her rights. Miss Hughes talked about how well Amelie was doing, then it was time for Mrs Collins to speak.

'Sadly, Leo doesn't seem to be doing quite as well as his sisters. He's still very quiet at school and doesn't really socialise with his peers. It's hard for me to say how it would affect him if his sisters were adopted,' she sighed. 'He's a very troubled, vulnerable young man, and I can imagine it would be very difficult for him.'

Finally, it was my turn to talk. I wanted to be honest and open about how I felt. I took a deep breath and started to tell them what I thought.

'While I do fully understand the reasons behind separating the siblings and placing Amelie and Lexie for adoption without their brother, I'd like it to go on record that I am very much against a split adoption,' I told them firmly. 'Having cared for these children for three months, I've seen time and time again how much Lexie and Amelie depend on their big brother to provide them with security and comfort, and how much Leo adores his little sisters. I think we should do our very best to keep the three of them together.

'If the girls are adopted and Leo isn't, the consequences will be devastating for all three of them, but particularly for Leo. I worry that he'd never get over it and it would have a really negative impact on his mental health.'

Paula nodded and made some notes.

'Maggie, I think everyone here today understands where you're coming from,' she said sympathetically. 'You know these siblings and the bond between them better than any of us. But while I do take your points on board, looking at this independently, I agree with Alex that we have to give the girls a chance at having their own family. I believe that it's in Amelie and Lexie's best interests to split the sibling group up. The girls will still have each other, but not their brother.'

It was the outcome that I'd expected, but it still didn't stop my heart from sinking.

Paula turned to Alex.

'Do you know if there are any families willing to take on two girls?' she asked.

'I've spoken to the family-finding team and they know of at least three couples who would be open to adopting two girls of this age,' Alex replied.

'Maggie, if for some reason adoption doesn't work out for the girls, would you consider having all three of them long term?' asked Paula.

'Yes, I'd be delighted to,' I said. 'In my opinion that's the best option for the children.'

'What about Leo?' she asked. 'Would you be willing to have him on his own as a long-term placement?'

I shook my head. I'd already given this a lot of thought.

'I don't think it would be fair to look after Leo on his own without his sisters,' I told her.

If two siblings left and one remained with me, I knew it could cause all sorts of additional problems.

'If Leo stays with me, the girls might see it as me rejecting them. I think you have to be seen to be doing the same for all three of them, and therefore it would be better if they all have a fresh start.'

I also knew that my home would be a permanent reminder to Leo of what he'd lost. There needed to be a plan in place for him so he knew that he was equally important to his sisters and didn't feel like he was being left behind. I wanted him to feel that he mattered too.

The meeting wrapped up soon afterwards, and finally I had the house to myself again. As I started to clear up, I felt an impending sense of dread in the pit of my stomach. Normally after a review meeting, I was left with a feeling of relief and a sense of joy that the right decision had been made and we could move forward with a long-term plan for the future of the child I was fostering. But the outcome of this morning's meeting was the last thing that I'd wanted. It was so hard knowing that my views weren't enough to change anything.

I flopped down on the sofa and burst into tears of anger and frustration. I felt such a deep sense of sadness for all three of them and what they were about to lose. And then came my biggest worry of all – how on earth were we going to tell them?

TWELVE

Breaking the News

Normally when it's decided that a child is going to be adopted, we begin by talking excitedly about forever families and reading books about adoption to get the child used to the idea. In the past, it had always been a very upbeat and positive experience, full of questions and intrigue. But how on earth were we going to tell the children that only two of them were going to be adopted? How would we explain to the girls that their beloved big brother wasn't going with them? And how could we tell Leo that his little sisters were moving on to a new family without him?

It was the worst possible news to be breaking, and the mere thought of it made me feel ill.

Alex and I talked about it at length on the phone the afternoon following the review meeting.

'Ultimately, it's down to me to tell them, Maggie,' she explained. 'As the children's social worker, it's my job to talk to them about this. I know how strongly you feel about it and you don't even have to be in the same room if you don't want to.'

'I want to be there,' I sighed. 'I know these kids better than anyone and I think I need to be there when they're told, especially for Leo. I want to be there to help pick up the pieces.'

I was adamant that we needed to tell him first.

'I promised him that when you and I had any information, he would be the first to know about it,' I told Alex. 'Plus, he's older so he's going to have much more of an understanding than the girls.'

'Do you think we should do it in conjunction with the therapist at CAMHS?' Alex asked.

I shook my head.

'So far he's refused to open up to her at all so I don't think having her there would help.' I told her 'It needs to be me and you. He deserves to know the truth first. Then we can break it to the girls,' I continued. 'The sooner the better, I think.'

Alex arranged to come round after school that evening.

'It's going to be OK, Maggie,' she told me. 'They might handle it better than you think.'

'The girls might,' I sighed. 'But Leo is a different matter. I know he's going to be completely devastated.'

I felt weepy all day just thinking about the conversation that we were going to have with them later that day. I tried to distract myself by doing some paperwork when Lexie was at nursery, but I couldn't concentrate on anything. After I'd been to collect her at lunchtime, I took her to the park but nothing stopped my mind from whirring. By school pick-up time, my stomach churned, both with nerves and dread at what was to come.

Alex was already waiting on the doorstep when I pulled up in the car with the girls. I knew Leo would be arriving home soon.

I got the girls a snack and got them settled in front of the TV in the living room to give Alex and me some time to talk to Leo. He arrived home ten minutes later.

'Alex has popped in for a chat,' I told him, trying to keep my voice light.

Leo looked suspiciously at us as we sat down at the kitchen table with him. As I poured him a cup of juice, I realised my hands were shaking.

I cleared my throat nervously.

'Remember I promised you that if we had any news about what was going to happen to you that we'd tell you first?' I said.

Leo nodded.

'Well, Alex and I need to talk to you about something.'

'OK,' he said, anxiously. 'What is it?'

As Alex began to speak, I couldn't bear to look at Leo. My heart was hammering in my chest.

'My manager and I have been talking about what's going to happen to you in the long term,' she told him. 'And we've decided that because the girls are still quite young, we really want to find them a new mum and dad so they can be adopted.'

'I don't want a new mum and dad,' snapped Leo.

'We didn't think you'd want that either, which is why we think it might work better to find a family for the girls so they can be adopted, and then find a different family for you; perhaps a long-term foster family.'

Leo looked confused as he struggled to process what Alex was telling him.

'What does "adopted" mean?' he asked.

'It's where people apply to the courts to become a child's new parents by law,' Alex explained. 'So they will live with them and take them on holiday and get to make decisions for them as if they were their own children.'

'But I don't want us to be adopted,' Leo said, looking confused. 'Why can't we all just stay here with Maggie instead?'

He didn't fully understand what Alex was telling him. I swallowed the lump in my throat as Alex tried to explain it as simply as possible to him.

'Leo, this is the plan for the girls,' she told him gently. 'Our plan for you is to find you somewhere else to live, maybe with another foster carer.'

He looked confused. 'So I'm not being adopted?'

Alex shook her head.

'We don't feel that it would be the best thing for you at your age,' she told him.

'But Lexie and Amelie are?'

Alex nodded.

Leo looked panicked now. 'But we'll still get to live in the same house together, won't we?' he said, his voice tinged with desperation.

'You'll live in different houses,' Alex told him gently. 'The girls will live with their adoptive parents and you'll live with your new foster family.'

I could see the panic on Leo's face now as the truth finally dawned on him.

'But that's not fair,' he yelled. 'You can't split us up. I need to be with my sisters. And they need me!'

I hated to see him so distressed.

'I know you do, flower,' I said sympathetically, putting my hand on his arm to try and calm him down.

He shrugged me off and began chewing on his lip like he did when he was stressed. I could see the skin starting to bleed.

'I know this is so hard for you to hear, Leo, but a group of us met and we talked about it long and hard to make sure we were doing the right thing and we all decided this was the best thing to do for all of you,' Alex told him gently.

'I've changed my mind,' Leo told her desperately. 'I don't mind being adopted. I'll get a new mum and dad too and then I can stay with Amelie and Lexie.'

Alex shot me a panicked look.

'The trouble is, Leo, we don't have many people who have the availability to adopt older children,' she told him. 'Most people are only able to take on one or two children at most, and as much as we'd have loved to have kept you all together, it's just not going to be possible, I'm afraid. It's been a really hard decision, but we feel that this is what will work best for all of you.'

Leo looked completely shell-shocked as the reality of what was happening sunk in. This was his family. Amelie and Lexie were all he had left.

'It's not fair,' he yelled. 'Mum didn't want me. Now you're taking away my sisters too.'

'Your sisters will always be your sisters, flower; no one can ever take that away,' I told him. 'I know this is so hard for you, Leo, but you'll build a new family of your own with the people that we find for you.'

His anger gave way to despair and he put his head in his hands and wept. His body shook with sobs. All I could do was put my arms around him and try my hardest to make him feel less alone.

Alex looked helpless.

'You go and talk to the girls,' I said to her quietly.

My heart broke for Leo as he sobbed in my arms. There was nothing to say. I knew there wasn't anything I could do that would make this better or take away his pain.

In the living room, I could hear Alex talking to the girls.

A few minutes later, I could hear little feet running through to the kitchen.

'I'm going to tell Leo that we're going to get a new mummy and daddy,' Amelie squealed excitedly.

She ran into the kitchen and looked puzzled when she saw Leo sobbing in my arms.

'Leo, why are you sad?' she asked, cuddling into him. 'Don't you want us to have a new mummy and daddy?'

He was too choked up to answer her.

'It's a lot for Leo to take in at the moment so he's just feeling a little bit sad,' I told her. 'And sometimes when you feel a bit sad you need a cuddle, don't you, Amelie?'

She nodded.

'You go back in and talk to Alex and I promise I'll come and see you in a minute,' I told her.

Amelie hesitated, then ran back to the living room.

Leo pushed my arms off him.

'She doesn't even care,' he raged. 'She and Lexie aren't even bothered that they're not going to live with me any more.'

'Leo, they're only little,' I told him. 'They don't understand what all this really means yet.'

'Well, I do,' he snapped.

He got up off his chair and stormed out of the kitchen. I ran after him as he stomped off up the stairs.

'Leo, are you safe?' I asked him.

'Stop asking me that stupid question!' he yelled.

A few seconds later I heard the slam of his bedroom door. I decided not to go after him straight away to give him some time to cool off.

I went into the living room where Alex was with the girls. She looked at me quizzically.

'Leo's gone upstairs for a little while,' I explained.

'I've just been talking to the girls about how we're going to find them a new mummy and daddy,' Alex told me.

'And for Leo,' added Amelie.

'No, Amelie, can you remember what we said about Leo?' Alex reminded her.

'Oh yeah.' Amelie smiled. 'Leo's a big boy so he's going to get a different family to us cos he's older.'

'Yeah, and we might even get a dog and a house with a swing,' Lexie piped up.

'Or a cat,' said Amelie.

I could see the girls were excited. Both of them were too young to truly understand the implications of what was happening. The reality of being separated from their brother might not hit them until they were living with their new parents and they realised that he wasn't there. They wouldn't feel a sense of loss until the time came for them to actually leave Leo.

Ten minutes later I went upstairs to check on Leo. He was lying on his bed, his eyes red and puffy from crying. He looked exhausted.

'Will I ever see them again?' he asked quietly. 'Even though they're getting adopted, can I at least still see them?'

I knew I owed it to him to be honest.

'We would ask for that to happen,' I told him. 'Alex will explain to the people who adopt the girls how important your relationship is. But, ultimately, it's up to them whether they're happy for you to see Amelie and Lexie. And even if you do, flower, it's important for you to realise that it's not going to be every week.'

'How often will it be?'

'Maybe once or twice a year,' I told him honestly. 'But you'll still get to visit your sisters and see how they're growing up. Amelie and Lexie won't ever forget you, Leo.'

His face crumpled and he started to cry again.

It felt so cruel having to do this to him after everything he had endured. As awful as it was, he needed to know the reality. Even if Social Services pushed for the adoptive parents to stay in touch with Leo, it was entirely up to them. I knew from stories I'd heard from other foster carers that during the adoption process, adoptive parents might promise letters and visits, but when they got their child, they were eager to start a new life, and it was their prerogative to change their minds. Sometimes adopters want to forget the children's pasts and move on with their lives, starting afresh.

'I know this is so hard for you, Leo,' I told him. 'There's nothing I can say that will make you feel better.'

He looked at me, his blue eyes filled with hurt and pain.

'I just don't understand why they're doing this to us,' he sobbed. 'Why can't we stay together? They're my sisters. They're my family. I can't lose them too.'

I find it very difficult to hold eye contact with children when I'm talking to them about a decision I don't agree with.

I knew everything that Leo was saying was true, and all I could do was to give him a hug.

'Like Alex said, a group of professionals got together and they talked about what they thought would be best for you, Amelie and Lexie, and they decided that this was the right thing,' I reminded him.

'It's not because they decided you needed to be away from your sisters or that you shouldn't be with them. Everyone knows that you've done an incredible job looking after them for so long, but they really feel this is your time now. You deserve someone to look after you, and so do Amelie and Lexie. You've got lots of things you need to work on, Leo, and you deserve the time and space to be able to do that, knowing that your sisters are being looked after really well.'

I was trying my hardest to approach it from the most positive angle I could.

'Well they've got it wrong,' he snapped. 'I just want to stay with them.'

It was impossible to know what to say because in my heart of hearts, I agreed with him.

'I'm going to tell them that I don't want Amelie and Lexie to be adopted,' he babbled. 'I'm going to stop them from taking them.'

'I'm afraid it's not your choice, flower,' I told him. 'Social Services have decided this is the right thing for all three of you. I know you don't like it and you're entitled to tell them what you feel, but I don't think you're going to be able to change anything.'

'When will they go?' Leo asked in a quiet voice.

'I don't know,' I told him. 'I know the family-finding team are going to start looking for a family and as soon as they've found somebody, Alex will come and tell us. Often, she'll bring a book with lots of photographs in of them and their house.'

'Will I see the book?' he asked.

'Of course you will. You'll need to see where your sisters are going to live. You'll also get to meet the adopters.'

'What if I don't like them?' he asked.

'I'm sure you will,' I told him. 'Alex is going to make sure that she finds the best possible parents for your sisters.'

It was so hard for Leo. His sisters were downstairs jumping up and down with excitement about moving; meanwhile he felt like his world had collapsed.

'Why can't we all just stay with you?' he asked me, desperation in his eyes.

'Because Social Services have decided that the best thing for your sisters is to find them an adoptive family,' I told him gently. 'And they want you to have your own family too. I don't want to stand in the way of that.'

'Well it's stupid,' he cried.

Leo refused to come downstairs until Alex had left.

'How are you doing?' I asked him, when he finally joined us in the living room.

He shrugged.

Over dinner, all the girls wanted to talk about was their new mummy and daddy.

'I wonder what my new mummy will make us for tea?' wondered Amelie as she tucked into her fish fingers.

'Do you think she'll be able to paint our nails like Louisa?' asked Lexie.

Leo had hardly eaten a thing and he pushed his plate away angrily.

'You've already got a mum,' he snarled at the girls.

'That's true, Leo, you do all have a mum, but unfortunately she's not able to look after you any more so that's why we're going to find the girls a new mummy,' I told them gently, trying to keep my voice light for the girls.

'Yes.' Amelie smiled. 'And Alex is gonna choose us a really, really good one, she said.'

Leo looked gutted. It was so difficult to balance the girls' excitement with his upset and devastation. Every little comment they made about their new parents was like a dagger to his heart.

I spent the rest of the evening feeling completely on edge. I was desperately worried that Leo would try and hurt himself, so I deliberately put on a film to try and keep him downstairs for as long as possible while I got the girls to bed. When I came back down, I made him a hot drink and some toast as he'd barely eaten anything at dinner time. When the film ended, he stood up abruptly and announced he was going up to bed.

'Don't get cross, Leo, but before you go upstairs I need to ask you something,' I said to him. 'Are you safe or do you need a distraction?'

'Stop asking me stupid questions,' he snapped.

'Leo, you need to tell me,' I asked again. 'Are you safe?'

'Yes!' he shouted. 'Just leave me alone, OK? I'm going to bed.'

He stomped off upstairs. Even though he had told me he was OK, I knew how distressing the events of the day had been for him, and I was terrified they might trigger him to hurt himself again. I was on tenterhooks as I sat on the sofa, wondering when to check on him.

My heart was in my mouth when I knocked on his door ten minutes later. When there was no answer, I pushed open the door hesitantly, terrified of what I was going to find.

Leo was fast asleep in bed.

I gave a sigh of relief. He was exhausted.

I quickly looked around the room just in case to make sure there were no blood stains on his bedding or on any tissues. There was no sign of anything suspicious to suggest that he'd been self-harming.

By the time I flopped into bed myself, I was absolutely exhausted. But as I lay there, I was totally unable to sleep. All I could think about was Leo and the look of agony on his face when we'd told him that he was going to be separated from his beloved sisters. Finally, in the dark of my room, I sobbed my heart out. How on earth was Leo going to cope with seeing his sisters being taken away? I cried until my pillow was wet. I'd overseen countless adoptions over the years and almost all of them had been positive. I knew this was going to be the hardest one that I'd ever had to face and, in all honesty, I was dreading it.

THIRTEEN

A Family Affair

Spring sunshine was streaming into the kitchen, the radio was playing and I was frying eggs. After the awful day we'd had yesterday, I was doing my best to try and stay positive and show the children that for now, life was going to carry on as normal.

The girls were playing in the living room while I made breakfast and Leo wasn't awake yet. Even though it was a school day, I'd decided to let him sleep in as long as he needed after the trauma of the previous day. Just as I was finishing cooking the eggs, Leo walked into the kitchen. He looked pale and there were dark shadows under his eyes.

'How are you feeling, lovey?' I asked him gently.

He shrugged.

'I know you're probably still very upset and angry, but that's understandable,' I told him.

'I just wish I'd died in my sleep,' he blurted out.

I went and sat down at the table with him and put my arm around his shoulders.

'I know this must be all really overwhelming for you,' I told him. 'I can understand that you're scared about what's going to happen, but you will get through this, OK, Leo?'

He nodded.

'If you don't feel up to going to school today, then I completely understand,' I told him. 'I can give your teachers a ring.'

He shook his head. 'No, I want to go,' he said firmly.

I knew that school had always been his escape from his home life, and I thought that at least it would take his mind off things if he was busy in lessons rather than sitting at home feeling upset.

When I got back home after dropping everyone off, I made sure I recorded what he'd said in my notes and I also rang Alex.

'Do you think he's genuinely suicidal?' she asked me.

'I don't think so,' I sighed. 'I think he's feeling very sad and overwhelmed, but I'm keeping an extremely close eye on him.'

'Well at least he's verbalising how he feels rather than keeping it all in,' Alex said. 'That's a positive. Has he been self-harming?'

'Not that I know of,' I told her. 'I'm on constant alert and I'm trying to keep him downstairs as much as possible.'

After I'd finished speaking to Alex, I also called Leo's school to check that he'd made it in. I also spoke to Mrs Collins and let her know what had happened yesterday and asked her to keep a close an eye on Leo.

As much as I needed to support Leo over what was going to happen, it was also important that I started to try and prepare the girls for the adoption process. Over the next few days, I read books with them about adoption and families so that they would understand that families could come in all shapes and sizes.

'Some families have a mummy and a daddy,' I told them, as we flicked through the pages together one afternoon. 'Some might have a mummy on their own, or two mummies or even a daddy and a daddy.'

We didn't know yet who their adoptees would be, so it was important that they were prepared for every scenario. The girls seemed to enjoy looking through the book and talking about all the different sorts of families.

'Look, Lex, this family is just a daddy on his own,' Amelie told her, pointing at the page.

'Do you think we might get just a daddy, Maggie?' Lexie asked curiously.

'You might do.' I smiled.

'I think I'd like at least one mummy,' mused Amelie.

'Can I have a dog?' asked Lexie.

While this conversation was taking place, Leo was sitting at the table doing his homework. I'd purposely chosen to look at the book within his earshot so he could hear what we were saying while not being directly involved. I thought it was important that he was prepared too and knew what to expect. Although he wasn't looking at us, I could tell that he was listening intently to our conversation.

A week after the review, Alex came to see me.

'I've been chatting to the family-finding team and I think there are two couples that might be suitable for the girls,' she told me.

She'd arranged to go out and visit both of them.

'Gosh, that's quick,' I sighed. 'Normally it's weeks or months before you find anyone suitable.'

'The fact is the girls are very adoptable,' she told me. 'They're still young and at the moment they don't seem hugely affected by their past. And they're gorgeous little girls, Maggie.'

What she was saying was true; with their corkscrew curls and shy smiles, any potential adopters would look at a photograph of the pair of them and their heart would melt. In a way, it made me even sadder for Leo. Moody, troubled teens were definitely less photogenic than sweet toddlers.

Alex was also trying to organise some play therapy for Amelie and Lexie to help them understand that they were going to be separated from Leo, but she was struggling to find anyone with availability.

'The waiting lists are so long, I'm worried it could be months before they're seen and they'll have probably been adopted by then,' she sighed.

'Well, I've been reading lots of books with them and I can also do a bit of role play work with them with the doll's house,' I told her.

I'd sat in on enough play therapy sessions and read countless books to know a lot of the techniques to use with children.

'Thanks, Maggie, that would be brilliant,' replied Alex gratefully.

One night, my friend and fellow foster carer Carol invited Leo round to her house to have tea. She had taken on three children long term who I had originally fostered. Mary was ten, Sean was eight and Dougie was seven. Although the boys were a few years younger than Leo, we'd met up a couple of times at the park and they'd got on well, so Carol knew what was happening with Leo, Lexie and Amelie, and I jumped at the chance of having some time with the girls to talk about families without worrying about upsetting Leo.

'I know, let's play with the doll's house,' I told the girls when Amelie got home from school that afternoon.

I had one big wooden house and two little ones as well as lots of little figures. I wanted to use the dolls to reinforce the message that Leo wasn't going with them to their new home. Despite all the conversations around families, I wasn't sure the girls had yet realised that Leo wasn't going to be with them. In all honesty, I didn't think it would fully hit them until they had already moved in with their new family and Leo wasn't involved.

I got out all of the dolls from the house.

Amelie had a red headband on so I found a small piece of red ribbon and tied it around one of the doll's heads.

'This one looks just like you,' I told her. 'So this can be our Amelie doll.'

I did the same with Lexie – picking a doll that had a pony-tail like hers.

'So who can this one be?' I asked, picking up a male doll. 'Shall we have this man being your new daddy?'

The girls nodded.

'And this can be our new mummy,' said Amelie, pointing to another one.

Lexie picked up a doll with white hair and glasses that looked like a granny.

'This one's the Maggie doll,' she told me.

Charming, I thought to myself, laughing. Then we chose a doll to be Leo and I put all the dolls into the big house.

'Let's pretend this is our house – here we all are,' I told them. 'Oh, look your new mummy and daddy have come to visit our house.'

I got the figures and made them knock on the door.

'Hello, are Amelie and Lexie there? I'm their new daddy. Can they come and live at our house please?'

The girls giggled as I put on a funny deep man's voice.

'Look, Leo and I are waving goodbye to you,' I told them. 'Lexie, you hold the mummy doll and Amelie you hold the daddy and walk the four of you back to your new house over there.'

'Maggie, what's Leo doing when we go away?' Amelie asked.

'Oh, he's just eating his tea.' I smiled. 'Then he's going to watch a bit of TV.'

'What, in our front room?'

'Not in your front room,' I told her. 'You've got a different front room now because you're in your new house over there.'

'Oh yeah,' she said. 'Silly me.'

'What are you and Lexie doing in your new house?' I asked her.

'We're playing with our new dog,' replied Amelie.

'Woof woof,' laughed Lexie.

We were making a game out of this scenario, but at the same time it would get them used to the idea that Leo wasn't going to be with them in their new house.

In the role play I'd kept Leo at my house. In all likelihood, I knew he wouldn't be leaving at the same time as the girls because realistically it was going to take longer to find a carer for him.

That night after dinner I asked them: 'Shall we make sure the dolls are all tucked up in their beds?'

We put the doll Leo and me in our beds in the big doll's house. Then we put their new mummy and daddy in bed in their house and then Amelie and Lexie in their new bedrooms. The girls were really enjoying the game and I hoped that underneath their laughter, they were slowly starting to understand the reality of leaving their brother behind.

The first couple of times we played with the doll's house, we did it without Leo around. But a few days later, the girls naturally started playing with it themselves. Leo was watching TV in the same room.

'Look, Leo, I'm jumping on the bed with my new mummy at my new house,' said Amelie.

'And I'm on the swing in the garden with my new daddy,' added Lexie. 'But you're not at our new house.'

'Why are you saying that?' he snapped, tears filling his eyes.

He got up and stormed out of the living room. I followed him into the kitchen.

'I know it's hard for you to hear them saying things like that, lovey, but it's important that the girls understand what's going to happen to them,' I explained gently. 'They're only little so the best way of doing it for them is through play. They're not saying it to be mean or to upset you.'

'Well it's just stupid,' he hissed.

Every day felt like a constant juggling act. On the one hand, I needed to talk to the girls about adoption and get them used to the idea of going to live with their forever family. On the other, I was dealing with Leo's distress and upset, as well as trying to work through my own underlying belief that none of this should be happening at all. I felt like I was being pushed and pulled in different directions. It was important for the girls to talk about adoption and get them excited about their new family, but at the same time I didn't want Leo to think I was rubbing his nose in it and cause him any more hurt and pain. I'd never been in a situation like this before. In the past, sibling groups I'd fostered had always been kept together and I was finding it all very hard. To make matters worse, I knew it was only going to get more difficult when a new family was found for the girls.

As it happened, it took much less time than I expected. Normally for slightly older children like Lexie and Amelie, it could take several months to find a suitable family, but three weeks later Alex rang me.

'One of the couples seems ideal, Maggie,' she told me, sounding excited. 'I've got a good feeling about them and they seem very keen.'

She explained that their paperwork had been done and they'd applied for a date for them to go in front of a matching panel.

'Already?' I gasped.

'Well it's probably not going to be for another month or so, but we wouldn't be taking them to panel if we didn't think it was a good fit,' she replied.

I was shocked that things were moving so quickly.

'Honestly, they're both great, Maggie,' she reassured me. 'You're going to love them.'

I listened as she told me about the couple. Simon and Sally were in their late thirties and had been married for eighteen years. Simon was a carpenter and Sally had been a school dinner lady until she'd given up work to care for her mother who had cancer and had sadly died. They had two older sons: Steven, who was 16, and Damian, who was 15.

'Simon was adopted as a child and it's something they've always talked about doing,' Alex told me. 'Their boys are older now and Simon's just added an extension to their house so they've got a spare room. They're not particularly hung up on adopting babies and would rather take on a small sibling group and I think they've fallen in love with the idea of having two little girls.'

'They do sound perfect,' I agreed.

'While they're waiting for their panel date, they've asked to meet you to find out more about the girls,' Alex told me. 'Obviously, it's entirely up to you, Maggie. You don't have to meet them if you don't feel comfortable.'

'No, I'd like to,' I told her.

I was keen to meet them and find out what they were like. I also wanted to tell them more about Leo and for them to hear from me how important he was to the girls and to stress how much it would mean to all three of them to be able to keep in touch once the girls were adopted.

A few days later, when the children were at nursery and school, Alex came to pick me up. Simon and Sally lived in a town forty minutes' drive from me. I felt strangely nervous as we drove into a cul-de-sac and pulled up outside a 1960s brick semi.

'Here we are,' said Alex.

We knocked on the door at the side of the house and a tall, broad man with ruddy cheeks and ginger hair opened it. He was dressed in a navy jumper covered in sawdust and worn ripped jeans.

'Hello.' He smiled.

As I walked into the kitchen through the back door, he shook my hand vigorously.

'You must be Maggie,' he said. 'I'm Simon. Sorry, these are my work clothes. I'm not always such a scruff.'

'Oh, don't worry,' I told him, smiling.

'Something smells nice,' said Alex, sniffing the air.

'Oh, Sal's got some brownies in the oven,' he explained.

As soon as he mentioned her name, Sally appeared by his side.

'Hello.' She beamed. 'Lovely to meet you.'

She was a large, cuddly woman with a wild mane of long hair – in fact I noticed that she had similar corkscrew curls to the girls, which was nice.

'Come on in,' she said, leading us into the living room. 'The brownies will be ready soon.'

The house felt very warm and homely. There were lots of rugs, cushions, throws and ornaments and trinkets. Everything was mismatched and looked worn, but it also felt cosy and welcoming. My heart leapt when I saw a black collie curled up on the living-room floor.

'Oh, you've got a dog!' I smiled. 'The girls will be delighted. That was top of their wish list.'

We had a cup of tea and a homemade brownie and they listened intently while I told them all about the girls.

'They've settled with me really well and haven't shown a huge amount of loss in terms of their mother.

'They have a very strong bond with their brother Leo. He was the one trying to hold it all together at home when their mum was drinking or out with her boyfriend. He made sure

Amelie got to school and he stayed off school to look after Lexie when Mum was too out of it.'

'Poor lad,' sighed Sally.

'Yes, we feel very bad about not being able to take him too,' said Simon. 'But with the girls and our own lads as well, with all his issues we just didn't think we could manage it.'

'Don't worry,' Alex reassured them. 'Adoption isn't something we're looking at for Leo.'

I also wanted to warn them about what might be ahead.

'We're doing our best to prepare Leo and the girls for the separation but Leo's very vulnerable at present and I'm worried about how he's going to handle the whole settling-in process. He might try and make things difficult for you or be hostile when you come to the house.

'I wanted you to know it's nothing personal; it's just his way of working through it.'

'We really feel for him,' sighed Sally.

'My main hope for Leo is that he can maintain some contact with his sisters and perhaps see them two or three times a year,' I told them. 'How do you feel about that?'

Sally looked at Simon.

'Oh, of course.' He nodded. 'We'd be really happy for the girls to see him if that's what they want.'

'Maybe they could write to him or email him as well?' Sally asked, looking at Alex.

'Absolutely.' She nodded.

'I'm sure Leo would love that,' I added, smiling at them.

I felt so relieved that they at least seemed open to the idea of Amelie and Lexie keeping in touch with their brother, and meeting them both had set my mind at rest a bit.

'What did you think?' Alex asked me as I got back into the car.

'They seem really lovely,' I told her. 'I think the girls are going to like them.'

I was sure the girls were going to be fine. My main worry was how Leo was going to handle meeting them when the time came.

Six weeks later, Sally and Simon went to panel. Things had calmed down over the past few weeks. Leo was eating small amounts but regularly, and his bed-wetting had stopped. Much to my relief, I also hadn't seen any evidence of him self-harming. But now the panel date was here, I knew the wheels were in motion and there would be no avoiding what was going to happen.

Although it seemed extremely unlikely that Sally and Simon would be turned down, you couldn't assume anything until the court had officially matched them to the girls. The morning of the panel, I hovered nervously by my mobile waiting for Alex to ring.

The call came just after midday.

'All approved!' she told me happily. 'If it's OK with you, Maggie, I'll come round and tell the girls tonight after school and bring their books with me.' (Like all adopters, Simon and Sally had put together a book for each of the girls with lots of photos of themselves and their new house that they could look through before they met them.)

'Of course,' I said.

'Do you think Leo should be there when we tell them?' Alex asked. 'Or could you make other arrangements for him?'

I'd been mulling that one over in my own mind.

'I think it's important that he's there too,' I told her. 'It will be good for him to be able to see who's adopting his sisters and where they're going to be living. I also want him to feel like he's being kept in the loop with everything that's happening.'

Even though we were splitting them up, I didn't want Leo to feel that he was being pushed out.

I couldn't quite work out how I felt at this stage. I was excited for the girls, but I was also very apprehensive and worried about how Leo was going to handle the news. Having never worked on a split adoption before, this was a steep learning curve for me too and I just didn't know how Leo was going to react now it was becoming a reality. After a few weeks of stability, his biggest fear was now about to come true.

All three of them were having a snack in the kitchen when I heard the door go.

'That will be Alex,' I told them.

I went to let her in.

'Everything OK?' I asked her quietly.

'It all went brilliantly.' She smiled. 'They're really happy and excited.'

'Let's hope the girls feel the same,' I sighed.

Alex walked through to the kitchen, clutching two big books under her arms.

'Lexie, Amelie, guess what?' She beamed, putting on her best excited voice. 'I went to a meeting today and do you know what? We have found you a new mummy and daddy!'

I saw Leo's face drop.

'Oh, it's a mummy and daddy and not two mummies?' asked Amelie, clearly remembering all the books they'd been looking at.

'No, it's definitely a mummy and a daddy,' Alex said. 'And they've asked me to bring a book round to show you both so you can see pictures of them and your new house.'

The girls' mouths gaped open and they rushed over to Alex. Amelie practically ripped the book out of her hand and started flicking through it.

'Lexie, Lexie, there's a dog!' she shouted, showing her the photo.

Lexie jumped up and down with excitement.

'Woof woof!' she barked, giggling.

Alex tried to get them to sit calmly at the kitchen table with her and look through each page. I could see Leo watching intently from the other side of the room.

'Leo, do you want to have a look too?' I asked him.

'No!' he snapped.

But I could see that he was curious.

'This is your new mummy and daddy,' Alex told them, calmly showing them the first photo of Simon and Sally.

'The daddy's got orange hair,' yelled Lexie.

'Someone in my class has got hair like that too.' Amelie nodded. 'And the mummy has got curly hair like us.' She smiled.

They flicked through the rest of the photos of the house and the garden. They were excited that there was a football goal and a swing in the garden. Lexie lost interest after a while and she left her book on the table while she wandered off to play with some toys. I saw Leo surreptitiously pull the book towards him to have a look.

Meanwhile, Alex was still going through everything with Amelie.

'This is yours and Lexie's new bedroom,' she told her. 'And look, you've got a bunk bed to sleep in.'

'But where will Leo sleep?' Amelie asked, looking confused. 'Which one is Leo's bedroom?'

'Remember, Amelie, that we're going to find a different family for Leo,' Alex gently reminded her.

'Oh yeah, silly me.' She grinned, turning back to the pictures.

I saw Leo watching his sister intently, but it was impossible to tell what he was thinking.

'Here's another photo of your new mummy and daddy,' Alex continued. 'And these two boys are your new brothers, Steven and Damian.'

I saw Leo's expression shift to one of anguish, and I quickly stepped in.

'Leo, could you do me a favour and help me carry this washing upstairs?' I asked him.

He didn't say a word, but he did what I'd asked. We walked up to my bedroom and put it on the bed.

'Are they really going to get new brothers?' he asked me, looking close to tears.

I could see the devastation on his face, but I knew I had to be honest with him.

'Yes, there are two older boys at their new house,' I told him. 'And I know that must make you feel really sad.'

'They're not Amelie and Lexie's real brothers,' he sobbed. 'I am.'

'I know you are, sweetie,' I told him. 'And you always will be. Nothing's going to change that.'

Tears streamed down his face and I felt so cross with myself that I hadn't prepared him for this. I tried to put my arm around him but he shrugged me off.

'Leave me alone,' he snapped 'This isn't fair.'

The worst thing was, he was right. It wasn't at all fair that he was having to go through this, but it was going to happen and there was nothing any of us could do to stop it.

My heart broke for Leo and all the pain he was in and I felt tears prick my own eyes. I felt sick with dread at what was yet to come. We hadn't even started the settling-in process yet, and I could only imagine how painful it would be for him.

'I'd better go down and check on Alex and the girls,' I told him gently. 'Will you come down with me?'

He nodded, wiping his eyes.

'I'll go and watch telly in the front room,' he said. 'I've had enough of listening to them go on about new mummies and daddies.'

'Don't worry, Alex will be going soon,' I told him.

It was extremely hard to balance everything. The girls were so excited about their new parents and it was important they were allowed to talk about them. After Alex had left, the girls seemed to calm down a little, but Leo was still very, very quiet.

At dinner time he didn't eat a single thing, he just pushed the pasta around his plate.

He sat downstairs watching TV while I put the girls to bed. Both of them were full of excited chatter. Alex had told them they would be meeting their new parents the following day, and they could hardly contain their excitement.

Once the girls were in bed, I came downstairs to make a cup of tea and get Leo a drink of milk. The kitchen bin was almost full and needed changing, and as I dropped the tea bag into it, I noticed several ripped pieces of paper sitting on the top. I felt sick as I realised that it was a photograph that I recognised.

Amelie had taken her book up to her room, but Lexie's was still lying on the kitchen table. As I flicked through it, I found that there was a page missing and a jagged edge at the spine where it had been ripped out. The missing page was the photo of Steven and Damian; the girls' new brothers. The picture I'd found in the bin.

My heart felt heavy. I fished the pieces out of the bin, picked up the book and walked into the living room.

'One of the pages has been ripped out of Lexie's book,' I told Leo, keeping my tone casual.

Leo continued to stare at the TV, his expression unchanging.

'Oh, Lexie probably did it,' he said, still focusing firmly on the screen. 'She's always ripping things out of books.'

'That's a shame,' I said. 'Never mind. I think I can tape it together and stick it back in.'

I knew that Leo had done it, but I also knew there was no point in pushing it or telling him off. He had a right to feel sad and jealous about what was happening to his sisters and I knew I needed to let this go.

It was clear that the next two weeks were going to be an emotional rollercoaster. One way or another, we were in for a rocky ride and it was going to be tough for everyone.

FOURTEEN

First Meeting

That night I tossed and turned for hours, struggling to get even a wink of sleep. I felt mentally and physically exhausted after the challenges of the day, but no matter how hard I tried, I couldn't nod off. Every time I closed my eyes, I remembered the look of absolute devastation on Leo's face when the girls had been shown the photo of their new brothers.

I still felt so angry with myself for not preparing all of them for the possibility that the adopters might have other children. We'd talked about different types of parents, but not the fact they could have older siblings. Leo had been so shocked and hurt by it, and I felt guilty that I hadn't prepared him for this bombshell. Accepting Simon and Sally was one thing, but I had no idea how he would cope with the two older boys as well.

By 4.30 a.m., I admitted defeat and went downstairs. I made myself a cup of tea and sat at the kitchen table. Lexie's book was still sitting on the side and I sighed. Although I knew it wasn't right, I completely understood why Leo had ripped the photo out. To be honest, I was worried sick about him. He'd hardly eaten anything the night before. I'd put a bowl of grapes and a plate of biscuits out in the living room when he was watching TV in a bid to get something down him. He'd had a handful of grapes and one biscuit, which I supposed was better than nothing, but I knew it wasn't enough to sustain him. Now things were suddenly happening so quickly, I had to be on constant alert for any possible signs of him self-harming. It was a relief when I stuck my head into his room and found him asleep. I'd checked his room and the bathroom for any signs of blood, but thankfully there hadn't been anything.

By 6.30 a.m., I was showered, dressed and had had my breakfast. As soon as the girls woke up, they were both full of excited chatter about their new parents. When Leo came down to breakfast, he glared at both of them.

'Are we going to see our new mummy and daddy today?' said Amelie, as she tucked into her Weetabix.

'You are indeed,' I told her. 'Remember Alex said that she's going to bring them round after school for a cup of tea?'

'They're not going to be Leo's mummy and daddy though, are they?' she asked.

I knew she wasn't deliberately being mean. She was only five and she was just trying to get everything straight in her head.

'No,' he snapped. 'They're not going to be my mum and dad. I don't want a new family.'

'We want a new mummy and daddy though, don't we Lex?' Amelie asked. 'And we want a dog. There was a doggy in that picture, wasn't there, Lexie?'

Lexie, her mouth full of cornflakes, nodded.

'Maggie, do you think they'll bring the doggy with them today?' asked Amelie.

'Not today, flower,' I told her. 'But you can meet it when you go and see your new house.'

'What's the doggy called?' asked Lexie.

'You know what, I don't actually know,' I said. 'Did it say in your book?'

Amelie shook her head.

'Well then, you'll have to ask your new mummy and daddy what the dog's name is when they come round tonight.'

After they'd finished their cereal, the girls skipped off upstairs to play in their bedroom. Meanwhile Leo stayed sitting at the kitchen table, not saying a word. The piece of toast I'd put in front of him was untouched and had gone cold.

Normally, when we introduced children to their new parents, I made sure everything was happy, smiley and upbeat, but having another child involved who wasn't happy about it made it all so much harder. Every question and excited comment from his sisters must have felt like another kick in the teeth.

'Where am I going to be tonight when the people come?' he said in a quiet voice.

'Where would you like to be, lovey?' I asked him. 'Do you want to be here to meet Simon and Sally, or would you prefer to go to Carol's for an hour after school?'

He shrugged.

'Well why don't you stay here and see how you feel?' I suggested. 'If you're finding it difficult, you can pop round to Carol's. I could let her know that you might be coming.'

He nodded. I thought it was a good option and that way, if he was finding it all too much, he had a get-out clause.

After I'd helped the girls get dressed and dropped Lexie at nursery and Amelie at school, I returned home and gave my friend Vicky a ring. I'd kept her posted on everything that had been happening. My head was spinning and I needed to talk things through with another foster carer.

'How did telling the kids go?' she asked.

'Great and awful at the same time,' I sighed.

I explained how I was finding it hard balancing the girls' excitement with Leo's devastation.

'I messed up,' I told her, explaining his reaction to the fact that the girls would have two older brothers. 'I feel like I've let him down,' I sighed. 'I knew there were two older boys and I should have prepared Leo for the possibility of that.'

'You can't prepare them for every single scenario, Maggie,' she said. 'You're in unchartered territory, remember? You've never done a split adoption before so this is all new to you. You're doing the best you can.'

'But I still made a mistake,' I sighed.

'You're human,' she told me. 'We all get things wrong sometimes. You can't beat yourself up about it.'

'I just feel so responsible for Leo. I can see how much he's hurting and I've just made it worse.'

'Well it sounds like the girls are happy, which is great,' Vicky said. 'I hope their first meeting goes OK later.'

'So do I,' I agreed.

In between meeting Simon and Sally for the first time and them going to panel, I'd already sat down with Becky and Alex and mapped out the settling-in process and how we were going to do it. We'd agreed that it would be best to do it gradually over two weeks to give everyone time to get used to the idea. This week involved Simon and Sally meeting the girls and spending time with them at my house. The following week, they'd be taking them to their house, moving their things over and taking the girls on trips out. I also knew that at some point I needed to sit down with Leo and explain how the settling in was going to work so that there were no surprises for him.

My heart sank when I went to empty the laundry basket and found Leo's sodden sheets stuffed in there. His bed-wetting was back, a clear sign of his anxiety and distress.

The dog was still the main topic of conversation when I picked up Amelie from school later that day. Lexie was still too young to really understand what was happening so she hadn't said much to me about it after nursery.

My heart was in my mouth as I drove them home, wondering when Alex, Simon and Sally would arrive. Leo tended to get home fifteen minutes after us, and I hoped that the girls would at least have a little bit of time to meet their new parents first without him being there.

As soon as we got in, I headed to the kitchen and flicked the kettle on. Just as it had come to the boil, there was a knock at the door. I opened it to find Alex and a nervous-looking Simon and Sally standing on the doorstep.

'Hi, said Maggie,' smiled Alex. 'We saw you all getting out of the car.'

'We're not too early, are we?' asked Sally nervously.

'No, not at all – come on in,' I said, smiling.

I could see they'd both made a real effort. Simon was wearing a shirt and smart jeans and Sally had on a long skirt and jumper and was wearing lipstick. The girls had clearly heard the door and they came running into the hallway.

'Amelie and Lexie, this is your mummy and daddy,' I told them, making sure I dropped the word 'new'.

The girls hung back shyly.

'Aren't you going to come and say hello?' Alex encouraged them.

Amelie stepped forward.

'We don't know what the dog's called,' she told them. 'It didn't say in the book.'

For a moment Simon and Sally looked taken aback by the question, but they both laughed.

'Hello, Amelie,' said Sally in a kind voice. 'Our dog's called Trixie.'

'Is it a boy doggy or a girl doggy?' asked Lexie, moving closer towards them to join her sister.

'Trixie's a girl dog,' Sally told them. 'She's a collie dog and she's very friendly and likes licking people.'

'Yuck,' grimaced Lexie, and Amelie giggled.

'Maggie, the dog's called Trixie and it's a girl,' Amelie said, turning to me, even though I was standing next to them in the hallway and had heard every word.

'Well at least we know now.' I smiled. 'And that's a very good name for a dog.'

I led them all into the living room and Simon and Sally sat down on the sofa.

'Would you like to see another picture of Trixie?' Sally asked them. 'I took one on my phone yesterday.'

Both girls nodded excitedly.

Sally got her phone out of her bag and the girls knelt down on the floor and looked through her photos.

Thank God for that dog, I thought to myself.

It had been a great ice-breaker and had given the girls something to talk about.

'Amelie, why don't you go and get your photo book,' I suggested. 'I know you had lots of questions and now your mummy and daddy are here, they can answer them.'

She rushed off and got her book from the kitchen, then sat on the sofa with Lexie, Sally and Simon. As they leafed through it, they asked endless questions about the dog, the car, the swing in the garden and what they kept in the garage. Sally and Simon answered all of them while I said goodbye to Alex, who had to go to a meeting at Social Services.

'What's that jar on the side in the kitchen?' Lexie asked.

'That's our biscuit jar,' Simon told her. 'Can you guess who eats all the biscuits in our house?'

'Trixie?' guessed Amelie.

Simon shook his head.

'Your big brothers Steven and Damian eat all the biscuits,' Simon told them. 'And there's never enough left for me.'

'We've got another big brother too,' Amelie told him.

'Yes, we know.' Sally smiled. 'We've heard about Leo.'

'But he's not coming to our new house,' added Lexie sadly.

'Leo's going to get a different family just for him, isn't he?' I smiled.

Just then I heard a key in the door.

'Talking of which, that'll be your big brother now,' I told them.

I saw Sally shoot Simon a nervous look as I got up and went out into the hallway.

Leo looked apprehensive as he walked through the front door.

'Are they here?' he asked nervously and I nodded.

'Why don't you come and say hello?' I suggested in a low voice.

'No,' he scowled. 'I don't want to. I don't want to see them.'

Just then Simon popped his head around the living-room door.

'Hello, mate, how are you?' he said. 'I'm Simon and my wife Sally's in there with your sisters. I hear it's you we've got to thank for looking after these girls so well.'

Leo looked taken aback and didn't say anything.

'Leo, I'm just going to make everyone a cup of tea. Do you want to come and get a drink and a snack?'

He followed me through to the kitchen.

'How does he know I looked after the girls?' he asked.

'Leo, everybody knows how well you looked after your sisters and what an amazing job you've done with them,' I told him.

I sat with him at the table while he had a drink. He was extremely quiet, but I could tell that he was intrigued and was clearly listening to every single word coming from the front room.

'Why don't you make a start on your homework?' I suggested.

I wasn't deliberately keeping him out of the front room, but I thought it would be good for him to have a distraction, as well as giving Simon and Sally time on their own with the girls.

While Leo got on with his homework, I folded up some washing. Five minutes later, I popped my head around the living-room door. Amelie and Lexie were showing Sally and

Simon the photo albums I'd put together for each of them while they'd been at my house.

'Can I interest anyone in another cup of tea?' I asked.

'Oh, yes please,' said Sally.

'Look, Maggie, I'm showing them that time I swung really high on that swing and my shoe fell off,' Amelie told me. 'Remember when you took that picture, Maggie?'

'Oh yes.' I smiled. 'That was when we had a day out at the farm.'

Even though they'd only been with me for five months, I always made sure I took lots of photos and printed them out on the computer every few days so they'd always have memories from being at my house.

It was good to see that both girls had perched themselves in the middle of Sally and Simon. Amelie was showing them all the photos and Lexie was holding Sally's phone, still looking at pictures of the dog.

I went back into the kitchen. Leo was still sitting at the table, staring into space.

'How are you doing?' I asked him. 'I know this must be really hard for you.'

'I'm fine,' he snapped. 'I'm just doing my homework like you asked me to.'

I didn't want to push him to talk so I got on with making the drinks.

'Right, I've got two cups of tea here and some juice for the girls, so do you want to carry the plate of biscuits into the living room for me?' I asked him.

I knew Leo was curious about Simon and Sally and I thought giving him a job might encourage him to go in and see them.

'OK,' he huffed. 'If I have to.'

He walked into the living room with his head down and quickly put the plate on the coffee table.

'Nice to meet you, Leo,' said Sally but he just ignored her and went out.

'Are they staying for tea?' he asked when we went back into the kitchen.

'No, they're only going to be here for another ten minutes today,' I told him. 'But they'll probably eat here when they come back tomorrow.'

'They're coming again?' he gasped.

'Yes, flower,' I told him. 'Remember I told you they're going to be doing something with the girls every day for the next two weeks so they can all get to know each other.'

Leo rolled his eyes and exhaled dramatically, looking furious.

Ten minutes later, I went into the living room and told the girls to say goodbye.

'Simon and Sally have got to go now, but we'll see them tomorrow,' I said to them.

They quickly waved goodbye and ran into the kitchen to see what Leo was doing.

'How did that go?' I asked Sally and Simon, once the girls had gone.

'Oh, they're such lovely girls,' said Sally, clearly smitten already. 'Really sweet and chatty.'

'Is Leo OK?' asked Simon, looking concerned.

'Yes, he's fine,' I reassured him. 'Sorry that he was a bit frosty. He's finding this all quite difficult.'

'Of course.' Sally nodded. 'It's only natural.'

'We're just so sorry that we couldn't take him too,' sighed Simon, looking upset.

They were such nice people and it was a relief to see that they were concerned about Leo, as well as Lexie and Amelie, as it showed me they cared about his feelings and knew how important he was to the girls.

'Don't worry about it,' I told them. 'Just enjoy getting to know the girls.'

The next day, Alex had given permission for Amelie to leave school early so she could have lunch with Simon and Sally at our house. Then she and Lexie were going to spend the afternoon with them. I wanted to do it without Leo around so he didn't feel like it was being shoved in his face. The girls needed to have time on their own with their new parents without Leo being upset.

Lunch went well, and Sally and Simon stayed with the girls while I went to pick up Leo from school.

'Where are the girls?' he asked as soon as he got in the car.

'Simon and Sally are with them at the house,' I told him. 'I thought it would be a good opportunity for you and I to go and buy you some new trainers without the girls moaning about being bored and hungry.'

'OK,' he replied, though he didn't look too happy about it.

Leo didn't say a word until we pulled into the car park at the shopping centre.

'Do the girls like those people?' he asked me suddenly.

'I think so,' I told him. 'It's going to take a bit of time for them to all get to know each other but so far it's going well.'

I paused.

'What do you think?' I asked him. 'Do you like them?'

He shook his head. 'I hate them,' he spat angrily. 'They're stupid and annoying and really, really boring.'

'Do you really think you hate them, or maybe you just hate the idea of them?' I asked gently.

Leo looked puzzled.

'The girls seem to like them and that's good enough for the moment,' I told him. 'Maybe in time you'll get to know them and change your mind?'

'No way,' he snapped. 'I won't ever like them.'

It was awful seeing him so distressed, and I wished there was something I could do to ease his pain.

'You might never like the idea of your sisters going to live with them, and it's OK to feel like that, Leo,' I told him. 'But I'm afraid this is going to happen whether you like it or not.'

Before I could say anything else, Leo got out of the car, slammed the door and marched across the car park. I could totally understand his anger and I knew it was a reaction to cover up how desperately sad and helpless he felt.

That night I phoned Alex as promised to update her on how the settling in was going.

'So far, so good,' I told her. 'The girls seem really happy. They didn't object to me leaving them on their own with Simon and Sally and they all seemed to have a really nice afternoon together.'

'And how's Leo coping?' she asked.

'Not too well,' I sighed. 'Understandably he's finding it very difficult and he's been very frosty with Simon and Sally.'

Alex paused.

'Maggie, do you really think the settling in is going to work with Leo around?' she asked. 'Are we asking too much of him? I don't want his behaviour to jeopardise the girls' adoption.'

'What's the alternative?' I asked.

'We move him to another carer ASAP,' said Alex matter-of-factly. 'I'm sure I could find a short-term foster carer for him while we sort his long-term plan.'

My heart sank. I knew that would be the worst possible thing for him and his mental state.

'I can't do that to him, Alex,' I pleaded. 'He already feels rejected and unwanted. It would totally destroy him if we suddenly moved him to another carer.'

I was adamant that I could manage the settling-in process and Leo's feelings.

'Give him a few more days and I'm sure he'll start to come round,' I told her. 'He's still only thirteen. He's bound to be angry about it. He's losing his sisters.'

I also reminded Alex that I had Carol and Vicky, who could help out from time to time.

'We will get through it,' I told her confidently. 'At least this way he has time to get used to the idea and say a proper goodbye to his sisters.'

I just hoped that what I was saying was true. From what Alex had said, if Leo's behaviour got any worse or more disruptive, he would have to leave.

FIFTEEN

Countdown

Picking up the black marker pen, I put a big cross on today's date on the calendar that was hanging on the kitchen noticeboard.

'Twelve more sleeps until you go and live with your mummy and daddy,' I told Amelie and Lexie excitedly.

'But that's a very long time.' Amelie frowned.

'I know it sounds it, sweetie, but it will go really quickly,' I assured her.

Amelie and Lexie bounced up and down with glee at the thought of moving to their new house. Meanwhile Leo stared sadly into his uneaten bowl of cereal. Every morning since the move date had been decided, I had marked off the date on the calendar and told Amelie and Lexie how many sleeps there were to go. Even though he didn't like it, it was important that Leo had that information too so he knew what was going on and could still feel he had some element of control. I also wanted him to be prepared because Simon and Sally would be here at the house in the evenings sometimes, giving the girls baths and putting them to bed.

'Can you remember what's happening today?' I asked the girls.

'My mummy and daddy are picking me up from school and then they're going to take me to the park and put me to bed,' Amelie announced proudly.

'And me too,' added Lexie, not wanting to be left out.

I saw Leo flinch as he heard his sister refer to them as 'Mummy and Daddy'. While the girls were busy getting their shoes on for school, I went and sat with him at the table and finished my cup of tea.

'I thought that maybe when Simon and Sally are here tonight, I could get Lexie and Amelie's tea all ready and then you and I could sneak off to the cinema,' I suggested. 'Would you like that?

'We can even grab a burger beforehand too if you like?'

Leo shrugged. His eating was so haphazard at the moment it would be a relief for me to see him wolf down a burger and chips.

I hoped he would agree. This way, Leo wouldn't have to be around too much when Sally and Simon were here and it would give them some time to be with the girls on their own.

'OK,' he sighed. 'I suppose it's better than staying here.'

Once I'd finished making spaghetti Bolognese for dinner, Leo and I drove to the local Cineplex. We had a nice night together, although Leo only picked at a burger and was so quiet, I had to drag practically every word out of him.

When we got back from the cinema, the girls had already gone to bed. Simon and Sally were downstairs waiting for us.

'Has everything been OK?' I asked them.

'They were as good as gold.' Simon smiled.

'I got my first hug tonight,' beamed Sally. 'Lexie threw her arms around me completely unprompted.'

'That's so lovely.' I smiled back.

'Did you enjoy the film, Leo?' Simon asked him.

'It was good, wasn't it?' I said.

'It was all right, I suppose,' he replied, rolling his eyes and walking out of the room.

'Sorry about that,' I told them. 'Please don't take his behaviour personally. He's dealing with things in the best way that he can.'

'It's not a problem, Maggie, we do understand,' said Simon.

'He's doing so well, considering,' said Sally sympathetically.

For the next few days, I decided it'd be easier for Leo if he went to Carol's after school when Sally and Simon came round. To my relief, the girls seemed really happy and as the days passed, I could see they were getting more and more affectionate with Simon and Sally. One afternoon, it was lovely and sunny so they all went off to the park after school. As I waved them off from the living-room window, I noticed Amelie reach for Sally's hand. A few seconds later they paused and I was confused. Had they forgotten something? Then I saw Simon crouch down on the pavement and Lexie jumped on him for a piggyback. I couldn't help but smile as I watched them walk down the street, Lexie giggling as she tickled Simon's head.

It was lovely to see them becoming more comfortable in each other's company. As I'd got to know Simon and Sally more, I'd also really got to like them. They seemed to understand that it was going to take time for the girls to feel comfortable with them, and they'd been patient and never tried to force that bond. It was lovely to see that it was happening naturally.

One night, towards the end of the first week of the settling in, I tucked the girls into bed.

'How many more sleeps?' asked Amelie impatiently as she clutched her favourite rag doll.

'Only seven now.' I smiled. 'Just one more week. Are you enjoying getting to know your mummy and daddy?'

She nodded. 'I like my daddy's orange hair and my mummy's got nice shoes,' she said firmly.

'And my daddy is very strong and pushes us really fast on the roundabout,' added Lexie.

'Well, that sounds brilliant.' I smiled. 'I'm so glad.'

Both of the girls seemed particularly taken with Simon and the idea of having a daddy, as they'd never really had one in their lives before.

Later on that same evening, I went to say goodnight to Leo. He must have overheard me talking to them.

'Why are Amelie and Lexie so happy?' he asked, looking crestfallen. 'Why aren't they sad about leaving me?'

'I know it's hard for you, but they're too young to really understand that they're leaving you,' I explained to him.

'They're caught up in dogs, bunk beds and a swing in the garden. Everything's new and exciting and it probably won't hit them until they actually go.'

'They just don't seem bothered about not seeing me any more,' he sighed.

The next day was Saturday and it was a day that I'd been feeling nervous about as Amelie and Lexie were going to meet their new big brothers for the first time. They were all going to a farm for the day. I had arranged for me and Leo to drop the girls off, as I thought it might provide a good opportunity for Leo to meet the boys if he wanted to.

The girls knew they were going to a farm, but I hadn't said anything about the boys until we were on the way there, as I knew it would be too much for Leo to bear if they were constantly talking about their new brothers.

'I think Steven and Damian are coming along today too,' I mentioned casually as I drove us there.

I made sure that I called them by their names in front of Leo, rather than refer to them as their new brothers.

'Yay!' Amelie grinned. 'We're going to meet our new brothers, Lex.'

I glanced at him in the rear-view mirror and I could see the devastation on Leo's face as he saw how excited his sisters were.

As we pulled up at the farm, I could see Simon and Sally waiting along with two strapping teenage boys. They were big lads and one of them had red hair like Simon.

'Leo, do you want come and say hello?' I asked him as I let the girls out of the car.

He shot me an angry look. 'No,' he hissed. 'I want to stay in the car.'

'That's fine.' I smiled. 'I understand.'

I walked the girls over and Simon and Sally introduced us to the lads. The girls smiled shyly at them.

'Hi, boys, it's lovely to meet you,' I said.

Like most typical teenagers, they didn't say much but gave me a brief hello, grinning at the girls.

'No Leo?' asked Sally, a concerned look on her face.

'He wanted to stay in the car,' I explained.

I arranged to pick the girls up later that afternoon, which gave Leo and me a chance to go shopping and have a quiet day together at home.

When we went back at 5 p.m. to collect the girls, there was no sign of them.

'I don't know how long they'll be, so do you want to get the football out of the boot and have a bit of a kick around while we wait?' I asked Leo.

He shrugged.

I sat on a bench while he messed about with the ball.

In an ideal world, I would have liked him to meet the girls' new brothers just so he knew everyone in their family, but I knew how painful it was for him, so I didn't push him. Hopefully it wouldn't affect him keeping in touch with the girls. When siblings who had been separated did meet up, it was never normally at either of their new homes. It was always somewhere neutral like a park or a zoo.

Ten minutes later, I saw Simon and Sally coming out of the farm entrance, Lexie and Amelie skipping beside them and Steven and Damian following on behind. Leo kicked the ball and it bounced away from him and over towards the two boys. One of the lads ran to it and kicked it back to him. Leo scowled, picked the ball up and stomped back to the car. The girls were busy saying goodbye to everyone and didn't seem to notice.

'Bye-bye, Steven and Damian,' Amelie called as she and Lexie waved to them out of the window as I pulled out of the car park.

'Did you have a nice time?' I asked them. 'What animals did you see?'

I was trying to steer them away from the topic of talking about their new brothers in front of Leo.

It was only when I put them to bed that night that I asked them about the boys.

'So what did you think of your new brothers?'

'They're really tall,' sighed Lexie. 'Almost as big as our new daddy.'

'And they drink Coca-Cola and go to big school like Leo,' said Amelie, clearly impressed.

The following week the girls were going to start spending time at Sally and Simon's house. As happy as I was for them, I was dreading it as I knew that it was really going to hit home with Leo. The reality that his sisters were leaving would sink in when they were missing from our house and he would realise that the girls really would be leaving. By this point, the girls had both had their last day at their school and nursery and said goodbye to their friends. They'd be starting at a new school when they moved to Simon and Sally's. Now they'd both left the school, they had no distractions and it meant they could spend the week with their new parents settling into their new house.

On the first day, I drove them over and was going to stay with them for a couple of hours. The girls had seen photographs of the house, but they were itching with excitement to see it for themselves. I expected them to be a little bit nervous or hesitant, but as soon as Simon opened the door to us, they ran inside excitedly. Sally gave them a quick tour and they raced around, looking in all the rooms while Simon made me a coffee in the kitchen. We could hear giggling coming from upstairs as the girls jumped on the beds.

'I don't think you need me here at all,' I laughed. 'I feel like a spare part!'

Much to my delight, the girls really made themselves at home. It was a warm, sunny day so they played in the garden with Trixie and Simon pushed them on the swing. Then they made brownies with Sally while I read my book in the front room. It was a relief to see that they felt so comfortable there.

I'd arranged for Vicky to call in for a coffee when we got back to my house later that afternoon. An important part of the settling process was for the girls to be able to share their excitement and talk about their new mummy and daddy with other people apart from me. I wanted them to be able to do that without having to worry about Leo and how he was going to react.

'So what was your new house like?' Vicky asked them as she sat at the table with a cup of tea. 'Did you like it?'

The girls told her about everything, from the dog to their bunk beds to the kettle in the kitchen that whistled when it boiled.

'Oh, it sounds wonderful!' She smiled. 'Can I come and live there too?'

Lexie shook her head. 'No.' Amelie smiled. 'It's just for me and Lexie.'

It was lovely to see them being so positive and excited about everything. I worried sometimes that I spent too much time thinking about Leo and not enough focusing on them. With an ordinary settling-in period, I would give the child leaving all my attention, but as things were, the girls felt almost like an afterthought in this process, and I often felt guilty. While they watched a bit of TV in the front room, Vicky and I had a coffee.

'Gosh, you've got no worries about those two,' she said. 'It's obviously going really well.'

'It is.' I nodded.

'And how's Leo doing?' she asked.

'He's OK,' I sighed.

There was a general surliness about him whenever Sally and Simon were around, but thankfully he hadn't had any major meltdowns or been rude to them and I was relieved that he had never taken his hurt and anger out on the girls.

Ten minutes later, Leo arrived back from school. He got himself a drink, then watched TV with Amelie and Lexie in the living room. I listened at the door to check they were all OK.

'We went to see our new house today, Leo,' Amelie told him.

'Did you?' He shrugged. 'Was it boring?'

'No,' she replied. 'It was really good. We've got bunk beds and I'm having the top one and we saw Trixie the dog and we throwed her a ball so she could catch it.'

I waited with bated breath to see how he would react.

'You like animals don't you, Am?' He smiled. 'It will be nice for you to have a dog.'

Whatever hurt Leo was feeling, he could never bring himself to be horrible to his sisters or take his pain out on them. My heart swelled with pride and admiration for him.

I left them to it and went into the kitchen to chat to Vicky. When I popped my head around the door fifteen minutes later, the three of them were still engrossed in cartoons. They were all cuddled up on the sofa together. Lexie was curled up like a cat on Leo's lap and Amelie was snuggled into the crook of his arm, sucking her thumb. They looked so cosy and contented.

As I walked back into the kitchen, I felt tears pricking my eyes.

'Maggie, what is it?' gasped Vicky, concerned.

'They look so comfortable and happy together,' I sighed, wiping my eyes. 'I know it's going to happen, but the thought of having to split them up in a few days' time is unbearable.'

I'd been so caught up in the settling-in process and juggling everyone else's feelings that I hadn't really had time to process what was happening myself.

'It must be exhausting for you, but you're doing the best you can and it will be OK. It will all be over soon,' Vicky consoled me, squeezing my hand.

'That's what I'm dreading,' I sighed.

As the days passed, the girls spent more and more time at their new house. One day they left after breakfast and Simon and Sally weren't bringing them back until later that evening. I used the time to start packing up their things.

'What's all this stuff?' asked Leo when he came in the door from school and saw the pile of boxes in the hallway.

'It's some of Amelie and Lexie's things so Simon and Sally can take them to their new house,' I explained.

'But they're not going yet.' He frowned. 'Why do they have to take it now?'

'They are in a few days' time, sweetie,' I replied gently. 'It's nice for the girls to take some of their things, so that when they go round there they have some of their own bits and pieces around them. It will make them feel more comfortable and at home.'

Leo looked like he was about to burst into tears. For the rest of the evening, he stared at the clock.

'What time are the girls coming back?' he asked me anxiously.

'I don't know what time exactly, lovey, but it won't be until later,' I replied. 'I know they're having tea and a bath at their new house.'

'It's not fair,' he snapped. 'I haven't seen them all day.'

Just after 9 p.m. there was a knock at the door. Simon and Sally were standing there with a sleepy-looking Amelie and Lexie in their arms.

'Sorry we're so late,' he apologised. 'We were playing snakes and ladders after tea, then they had a long bath and we read them a few stories.'

'Don't worry,' I told them. 'They're in their pyjamas so you can pop them straight into bed.'

'But I haven't seen them all day,' huffed Leo, standing behind me in the hall.

'Flower, it's late and the girls need to get to sleep,' I told him. 'You can quickly say goodnight and you'll see them in the morning.'

While Sally got the girls settled upstairs, Simon carried the boxes in the hallway out to the car. Then I said goodbye to them.

I went into the living room where Leo had been watching from the window.

'Why did you let him take their stuff?' he asked.

'Leo, I told you why,' I said gently. 'The girls are going in a couple of days and they need to start taking their things into their new home.'

Leo started furiously pacing up and down the living room. Up until now, there had been a few moments of stroppiness, but mainly he'd just been sad. Now though, I could see his sadness had suddenly turned to anger.

'It's not fair,' he raged. 'I don't want them to go. This is all your fault, Maggie. You're letting them take them.'

'Leo, lovey, let's sit down and talk about this properly,' I urged him.

'I don't wanna sit down,' he shouted. 'I want that man to bring Amelie and Lexie's stuff back right now.'

'I know it's really hard, but this is the way we do it,' I told him.

I could see it had all got too much for him and the realisation of what was going to happen in less than forty-eight hours had suddenly hit him.

'Why are you doing this to us?' he shouted. 'Why can't you just keep us all? I hate you, Maggie.'

I tried to be rational with him and calm him down. I knew he was angry and hurting and needed someone to blame.

'Leo, I can't keep you all here because it's not what Social Services wanted.'

'You're getting rid of the girls,' he snapped. 'So when are you getting rid of me then?'

'Leo, I'm not getting rid of anyone,' I explained. 'It's about giving you and the girls the chance of having a new family.'

I walked over to him and tried to put my arm around him.

'I know this is really difficult for you,' I soothed. 'This was always going to be the hardest part, but I promise you'll get through it.'

'Get off me,' he shouted, pushing my hand away. 'I don't wanna get through it.'

'Leo, as hard as it is, this is going to happen,' I told him.

'No!' he shouted.

Suddenly he marched over to the corner where the wooden doll's houses were. He picked up one of the smaller ones and hurled it across the room. Then he kicked the big house until the wood started to splinter.

'Leo, stop that!' I yelled. 'Those are not your things to break.'

But he was past the point of listening.

He kicked the houses again and again until the wood buckled and broke and then he stamped on them repeatedly. I'd never seen him like this before and he was out of control.

'Leo, please stop,' I begged. 'This isn't going to make you feel any better.'

He didn't stop until both doll's houses were in pieces on the carpet. Then he sank down to his knees and sobbed.

'I'm sorry, Maggie,' he wept. 'I didn't mean it.'

I knew I needed to let him cry it out so I didn't say anything. I sat down on the floor next to him and he curled up in my arms and sobbed his heart out.

'Please don't let them do this to me, Maggie,' he cried. 'Please don't let them go.'

All I could do was hold him in my arms. His sisters were leaving and there was nothing that either of us could do to stop it.

SIXTEEN

The Last Goodbye

Walking into the bedroom, I went over to the window and drew back the curtains.

'Good morning, you two.' I smiled. 'How are you today?'

Amelie and Lexie were wide-awake and were lying on their beds, a messy pile of books and toys scattered over their duvets.

'Shall we go downstairs and I'll get you some breakfast?' I asked them.

'I want my mummy to get my breakfast,' said Lexie, folding her arms crossly. 'You're not my mummy.'

'You're right.' I smiled. 'I'm not your mummy, I'm Maggie. But do you know what, Lexie, in one more sleep you're going to wake up in your new house and your mummy can get you breakfast every day.'

She was obviously aware that things were about to change and she was getting everything straight in her young head.

It was Amelie and Lexie's last day with me and we were all going to spend it together. I'd got permission from Alex to take Leo out of school for the next couple of days to enable him to have one last day with his sisters before saying goodbye the next morning.

'As it's your last day here today, we're going to do something really special,' I told them excitedly as I made the toast. 'We're going to a theme park.'

I wanted to give the three of them a shared experience and help take their minds off what was about to happen tomorrow. But most importantly, I wanted to give Leo a positive last memory of being with his sisters. I sometimes did a goodbye party for children when they were leaving, but in this situation it didn't feel right. Going to live with their new parents was a positive thing for Amelie and Lexie, but I knew that having a big celebration with other people when Leo was hurting so much wouldn't do him any good at all. It would have been rubbing salt into his wounds and would be too much for him to cope with. The most important thing was for him to be able to spend the whole day with his sisters rather than sharing them with lots of other people. I wanted to give him the best goodbye with them that I could think of.

As we walked through the turnstiles at the theme park, all three of their faces lit up when they saw all the rides.

'What can we go on?' asked Leo suspiciously.

'You can go on anything you want,' I told him.

None of them had ever been to a theme park before. Because the girls were only young, the rides they could go on were quite babyish, but Leo didn't seem to mind and he went on everything with them. They laughed and screamed as they whizzed around in spinning teacups and on a mini rollercoaster, then we all went on the bumper cars. I made sure I took lots of photos of the three of them so I could print them out for

Leo. The three of them were caught up in the moment and enjoying themselves so it made it easy for them to forget about everything that had been happening and just have fun together.

At one point, Amelie persuaded Lexie to go on the ghost train with her. The girls sat in a carriage together while Leo sat in the one behind them and I waited outside. When the carriages emerged from the tunnel a few minutes later, I could hear Lexie wailing hysterically. When the ride stopped, I ran over to her.

'What's the matter, sweetie?' I asked.

'It was too scary,' she wailed. 'I didn't like it.'

'Oh, you poor thing,' I soothed.

I put my arms out to pick her up but she shook her head.

'I don't want you, I want Leo,' she said firmly.

When Leo's carriage emerged from the tunnel she cried and reached for him. He quickly ran over to her and lifted her out.

'I didn't like it, Leo,' she sobbed, flinging her arms around his neck. 'It was scary.'

'It's OK, Lex,' he soothed. 'It's not real. Nothing's going to hurt you. I'll make sure of it.'

She buried her head into his chest and I could see her little body instantly relax. Leo was the only one who could comfort her so instantly like that and it made my heart break all over again that tomorrow we were splitting them up for good.

On the way home, we called at a country pub for tea as it would take us over an hour to drive home. I was delighted when Leo managed to eat a child's portion of pasta.

As we left the pub, the girls were chatting about all the rides they had been on and which was their favourite. Leo was walking next to me and he was deadly quiet. One glance at the look of utter despair on his face told me that after the loveliest day, the realisation of what was happening when we got back home had suddenly hit him.

'I don't want them to go, Maggie,' he whispered, his eyes filling with tears.

I put my arm around him. 'I know this must be so, so hard for you, flower, but you're doing brilliantly,' I told him.

'Will I ever see them again?' he asked, the tears spilling from his eyes.

'Simon and Sally have said they're happy for you to see the girls, so in a couple of months, when they've settled in, hopefully we can all meet up.'

'What date?' he asked. 'Can you put it on a calendar for me and put it up on the wall like you did with the girls?'

'I don't have a date, lovey, I'm afraid,' I told him. 'It's up to Simon and Sally. When they feel the girls are ready, then they will make it happen.'

Nothing was definite, but I had to trust that Simon and Sally would honour their promise and let Leo see his sisters.

By the time we got home, the girls were exhausted. I put the last few things of theirs into a case as they got into their pyjamas.

'Where's your case, Maggie?' asked Amelie. 'Have you and Leo packed up all your things?'

'Remember, sweetie, Leo and I are going to stay here and you're going to live with your mummy and daddy.'

'Oh yes, I remember now,' she sighed.

I went and sat on the bottom bunk with Lexie.

'Just one more sleep,' I told them both. 'Are you looking forward to living with your mummy and daddy and your new big brothers?'

They both nodded eagerly.

'And Trixie,' Lexie said, reminding me of the dog.

'Oh gosh, yes, we can't forget Trixie.' I smiled. 'I bet she can't wait to have you there.'

I gave them both a hug.

'Ooh, I'm going to miss giving you both cuddles night-night,' I said to them, tucking them in one last time.

My heart felt heavy as I went downstairs to see Leo. I could see how sad he was and I decided the best thing would be to keep him busy.

'We need to wrap the girls' presents,' I reminded him. 'Will you give me a hand?'

When the girls had gone to the farm for the day, Leo and I had gone shopping and he'd picked out two silver bracelets. They both had a disc on them and we'd had the word 'Sisters' engraved on the front and 'Love, Leo x' on the back.

'So they can remember me forever,' he'd told me at the time.

Now, Leo scowled. 'I don't want to help you wrap them,' he spat. 'You do it. I'm watching telly.'

I knew the realisation that they were leaving in the morning was all too much for him.

Later on, I went into his bedroom to say goodnight to him. He was lying on the bed, wide awake, staring at the ceiling.

'Remember you're not losing them,' I told him. 'They'll always be your sisters and you will see them again.'

'You don't know that for sure,' he snapped.

'Sally and Simon are good people and we have to trust them,' I replied.

That night I couldn't sleep. I tossed and turned, worrying about how all three children would cope saying goodbye to each other. I was absolutely dreading tomorrow.

★

The next morning came around too quickly. When I came downstairs, Leo was already up and dressed and getting out bowls and boxes of cereals for the girls. It was like he wanted to take control and look after them again like he had in the past.

'That's so helpful Leo, thank you,' I told him, letting him take charge.

Saying goodbye to his sisters was going to be so incredibly painful for him that there were times when I'd questioned whether it was even the right thing for him to be here when Simon and Sally came to get Lexie and Amelie. However, I knew that it was important for him to have that final goodbye; he needed and deserved that closure. It wouldn't have felt right to rush him off to school and for him to feel like he was being pushed out of the way.

The girls were so excited and nervous that they were both a bit hyper.

'What time are Mummy and Daddy coming?' Amelie asked, over and over, bouncing in her seat.

Normally, I tended to keep goodbyes quite short, but in this case, I wanted to make it slightly longer for Leo's sake so he could have a proper goodbye with Lexie and Amelie.

When Sally and Simon arrived, I invited them in. The girls rushed to meet them.

'We're coming to live with you today!' squealed Amelie, clinging to Simon's legs.

I saw Leo get up and close the door to the living room so he couldn't hear them.

'I know you are,' said Sally. 'We are so excited. Trixie's waiting at home and the boys will be back later.'

I went into see Leo in the front room. He was pretending to be engrossed in a programme about moving to Australia.

'Shall we give the girls their presents, flower?' I asked him.

He shrugged.

'Come on, they're in the kitchen with Sally.'

As soon as we walked in, the girls started giggling, grinning up at Sally and Simon.

'Go on then,' Sally whispered to them. 'Go and give it to him.'

'Leo, we've got you a present.' Amelie smiled.

She handed him a big fluffy teddy bear.

'We made it at Build a Bear just for you,' she told him proudly.

'And it's got us in it!' yelled Lexie.

He looked confused.

'Press its tummy,' Sally encouraged him.

He squeezed the bear and Amelie and Lexie's voices came booming out.

'We love you, Leo!' it said.

I could see he was choked up and doing his best not to cry so I quickly stepped in.

'A talking teddy bear!' I smiled. 'That's brilliant.

'And Leo's got something for you too.'

He handed them their parcels. The girls eagerly ripped them open and stared in amazement at the bracelets. I read out what was engraved on them.

'Leo chose them especially for you because you're his sisters and you always will be,' I told them.

'How lovely.' Sally smiled. 'They're absolutely beautiful.'

'Can I put mine on now?' asked Amelie.

Sally and I helped the girls to put their bracelets on.

'Thank you, Leo,' said Amelie, throwing her arms around him.

He didn't say anything but he bent down and cuddled her and Lexie tightly.

Just then, Simon came back into the kitchen.

'Well, I think we're all packed and ready to go,' he said.

The girls quickly rushed out to the hallway to get their shoes on and Sally went to help them.

'Come on then, lovey,' I told Leo gently. 'Let's go and wave them off.'

The moment that he'd been dreading for so long had finally arrived and the look on his face was one of pure panic.

When Amelie and Lexie were ready, I knelt down and gave them both a cuddle.

'I have so loved being able to look after you both,' I told them. 'And I'm going to miss you lots and lots.'

Then I turned to Leo and put my hand on his shoulder.

'Say goodbye to your sisters, flower, they're going now,' I told him gently.

I wanted him to know that I was here and I was right beside him.

Lexie reached up to him and he picked her up and she buried her head in his neck.

'Bye, Leo,' she said. 'I love you lots and lots.'

Then she wriggled free and ran off down the front path without a backwards glance. Then it was Amelie's turn.

Leo wrapped his arms around her and closed his eyes as he engulfed her in a hug.

'Ow, you're squishing me,' Amelie giggled.

He let go and she followed her sister down the front path to where they were both waiting by the gate.

'Just remember, I'm your big brother,' he called out to them.

The words choked in his throat and he could hardly get them out.

My eyes filled with tears, and I struggled to swallow the lump in my throat.

I quickly said my goodbyes to Simon and Sally.

'Good luck,' I told them, smiling. 'Enjoy every minute with your girls.'

'Thank you so much, Maggie,' replied Sally. 'We'll be in touch.'

'Bye, Leo, mate,' said Simon.

I looked across at Leo. His eyes were glassy with tears. I could see his whole body was trembling and he was biting his lip, trying desperately not to cry.

I gave him an affectionate rub on his back to try and bring him some comfort.

'You're doing so well,' I told him as we stood on the door-step together. 'It's nearly over now.'

We watched as Simon fastened the girls' seatbelts, then he and Sally climbed into the front seats of their Vauxhall. The girls waved at us through the glass.

'No!' Leo shouted suddenly, running down the path towards the car in his bare feet. 'Stop! You can't do this! Please, please don't take my sisters!'

Simon looked shocked.

'Leo!' I shouted. 'Come back in, please.'

'Don't go!' he yelled. 'Don't take them!'

I ran down the path towards him.

'Come on, sweetheart,' I said, trying desperately to usher him back towards the house. 'Let's get you inside.'

Simon looked concerned and wound down the window.

'It's OK, Simon, you go,' I gestured to him. 'I can handle this.'

Thankfully, the girls were chatting to Sally and hadn't noticed what was going on outside.

'Come on, Leo,' I urged him. 'Let's go back inside.'

I led him up the path and quickly shut the front door.

He ran into the front room and started hammering on the glass.

'Don't take them!' he yelled. 'Don't take my sisters!'

It was too late.

He let out a huge wail as the car drove off down the street.

'They've gone, sweetie,' I told him gently. 'I'm sorry. But I promise it's going to be OK.'

He let out a guttural cry and sank down to his knees on the carpet. I knew there was nothing I could do or say to make him feel any better. All I could do was hold him and let him cry it out.

We sat on the floor together for twenty minutes. After a while Leo's gulping sobs subsided and he looked exhausted.

'You have managed the last two weeks so well,' I told him. 'I'm so proud of you.

'Can I get you a drink of water?' I asked him.

'I don't want water,' he snapped. 'I want my sisters. Please, Maggie,' he begged, looking up at me pleadingly. 'You've been to their house. Can't you just go and get them?'

'Leo, sweetheart, they've gone,' I told him. 'They're with their new family now and there's nothing you or I can do about that. But hopefully you'll get to see them in a couple of months. I know you're angry and upset, but it will get easier.'

I felt so powerless being unable to console him. All I could do was let him know that I was there for him and I was hearing what he was saying. It was unbearable watching a child in such emotional pain. His sisters were his only family and no matter how nicely and smoothly we'd tried to do it, the horrible truth was that we'd taken them away from him and now he felt like he had absolutely nothing left. He'd been left behind and his pain was so raw, I honestly wasn't sure whether he would ever get over it.

Thankfully, Leo slowly started to calm down.

'I'm going to go upstairs,' he sniffed, wiping his face. 'I just want to be on my own for a little while.'

'OK,' I said. 'I'll make you a drink and bring it up to you.'

I went into the kitchen and made him a hot chocolate as I knew it was one of his favourites. I warmed up the milk and sprinkled a few mini marshmallows on the top, then carefully carried it upstairs for him. Leo's bedroom door was wide open but when I walked in, he wasn't there.

'Leo?' I called. 'Are you in the loo?'

But the bathroom door was open too and he wasn't in there.

Then I noticed that the door to the girls' bedroom was closed. My heart started racing. Still with the hot chocolate in my hand, I felt sick as I slowly pushed the door open.

The room looked so bare without the girls' things. There, curled up in the foetal position on the unmade bottom bunk was Leo. Blood was pumping out of his arm onto the mattress protector beneath him and there was something silver lying next to him on the bed. To my horror, I realised it was a pair of nail clippers that he must have pulled apart.

I dropped the hot chocolate and it fell to the floor, splattering the white walls with brown froth.

'Oh my God, Leo!' I screamed. 'What have you done?'

SEVENTEEN

A Change of Plan

Panic seared through me as I ran over to Leo. His whole body was shaking and I could tell that he was in shock.

'I'm bleeding, Maggie,' he mumbled. 'I can't stop it.'

I gently lifted up his arm to have a closer look. There was so much blood pumping out of it and smearing his skin that I was struggling to work out exactly what he'd done. I could see that he'd cut himself vertically on the inside of his lower arm. The skin had split open and I flinched when I realised that I could see the muscle beneath it.

Please don't let him have hit an artery or a vein, I prayed.

Taking a deep breath to try and calm myself, I ran over to the wardrobe and grabbed a pillowcase off one of the shelves. I wrapped it around Leo's arm and got him to press down hard on it with his other hand.

I knew I needed to get him to hospital and quickly. The nearest A&E was a ten-minute drive away and I thought it would be quicker for me to take him rather than have to wait for an ambulance.

'Come on, lovey, we need to get you to the hospital,' I told him.

'I don't want to go to hospital,' he murmured.

As quickly as I could, I gently guided him down the stairs and out of the front door. The pillowcase on his arm was already sodden with blood by the time I helped him into the front seat and fastened the belt across him.

As I turned the key in the engine and took the handbrake off, I realised that my hands were shaking.

'Am I dying, Maggie?' Leo whispered next to me.

'Don't be silly,' I told him. 'It's going to be OK.'

I desperately hoped I was right.

Please let the roads be quiet, I thought as I turned out of my street. It was the middle of the morning, so thankfully the traffic wasn't too bad. As I drove along, my mind was reeling as I struggled to take in everything that had happened in the past couple of hours.

I looked across at Leo, concerned. He'd gone quiet and was resting his head on the passenger window and I was terrified that he was going to slip into unconsciousness.

'Leo!' I said loudly, in a desperate bid to keep him awake. 'How are you doing, flower? We're nearly there now, just please hang on.'

'There's still so much blood, Maggie,' he whimpered, his voice sounding faint.

'Hang on in there, Leo,' I told him firmly. 'We're nearly at the hospital and they'll sort you out. Just keep pressing down on your arm,' I urged him. 'That will help.'

Inside I was panicking too, but I didn't want him to know that.

A few minutes later I pulled up into the hospital car park. It was normally impossible to find a space, but I saw someone reversing out and quickly drove in there. I'd worry about paying later; I knew I had to get Leo inside and quickly.

I got him to put his good arm around my shoulder and I practically pulled him across the car park and into the entrance of A&E. When the receptionist saw us staggering through the automatic doors and Leo's blood-stained clothes, she immediately called for help. A nurse appeared and ran towards us with a wheelchair. Leo collapsed into it gratefully and she took us straight through to a cubicle. I quickly explained to a doctor what had happened.

'I only left him alone for five minutes,' I babbled. 'I knew he was hurting but I didn't think he was going to do this. As far as I know, he's never cut his arms before but it looks really deep and it wouldn't stop bleeding.'

I felt so helpless. All I could do was stand back and watch while the team of medics got to work on Leo's arm.

'Are you OK?' a nurse asked me kindly. 'Do you want to come with me to a relative's room and I can get you a cup of tea.'

'No, no, I'm fine, thank you,' I told her. 'I want to stay here with him.'

There was no way I was leaving Leo now. I knew he'd lost so much blood and I felt sick with worry.

Please let him be OK, I repeated again and again in my head.

I glanced down at myself and realised with horror that my own clothes were covered in Leo's blood.

After what felt like a lifetime, the doctor came over to talk to me.

'It's a deep wound, but we've stemmed the bleeding and we're going to have to stitch him up,' he told me. 'He's a very lucky boy. He was millimetres away from hitting an artery.'

'Thank you,' I told him, my whole body sagging with relief that he was going to be OK.

I walked over to the bed to see Leo.

'How are you doing, sweetie?' I asked him, ruffling his dark hair. 'You gave me such a fright.'

Leo stared back at me, his eyes glazed and glassy. He looked like he was in some kind of a trance.

'Please don't let them take my sisters, Maggie,' he mumbled. 'Don't let them do this.'

The nurse must have seen the distress and confusion on my face.

'He's probably just in shock,' she told me gently. 'It's often how our bodies deal with trauma.'

He just kept repeating the same thing over and over again.

I didn't try to talk to him or say anything else and the nurse asked me to leave while she stitched him up. I went outside to sort out the parking and to quickly call Alex and let her know what had happened.

'Hi, Maggie, I was just about to ring you,' she said cheerily. 'How did it go with saying goodbye to the girls this morning?'

'Alex, I'm at the hospital with Leo,' I told her.

She listened in shock as I told her what had happened.

'Oh no, that's horrific,' she sighed. 'The poor lad. Is he OK?'

'Not really,' I told her. 'He's cut himself quite deeply so they're stitching him up now. There was so much blood I thought he'd hit a vein or an artery and that he was going to bleed out.'

'Oh, Maggie, it doesn't bear thinking about,' she shuddered. 'What on earth did he do it with?'

'He got a pair of nail clippers and pulled them apart,' I sighed. 'Honestly, Alex, I'd been round the whole house and locked away every possible thing that I thought he could hurt himself with. I never thought of nail clippers.'

'If somebody wants to hurt themselves, they will find anything to do it with,' Alex told me.

I knew she was right but I couldn't help but blame myself.

'I'm so sorry this has happened, Maggie, you must be really shaken up,' she told me.

'I am a bit,' I admitted. 'I'd better go now and check on Leo.'

As she put the phone down, Alex said she would come up to the hospital as soon as she could.

When I went back to his cubicle, Leo had been stitched and his arm was bandaged up. His eyes were closed.

'He's had some strong painkillers so he'll probably be very drowsy and just want to sleep it off,' a nurse told me.

Eventually a doctor came to see me.

'Physically he's going to be OK, but he's lost quite a bit of blood and I want him to see someone from the mental health team, so I think it's best if we keep him in at least for a couple of nights,' he told me.

Leo was still sleeping and as a porter wheeled him up to the children's ward, I walked up with him. An hour later, Alex arrived.

'Oh, Maggie!' she gasped as she saw my blood-stained clothes. 'How is he?'

'He hasn't said much and he's very drowsy. The nurse said he's probably in shock.'

I explained that they were keeping him for a couple of nights so I needed to go home and get him some things.

'Don't worry, I'll stay with him until you get back,' Alex reassured me.

The first thing I noticed when I opened the front door were the splatters of blood all the way down the carpet on the stairs. I shuddered, and hurried upstairs to get changed. As I walked past the girls' room, I glanced in and saw the empty hot chocolate mug still lying on the floor. I couldn't bring myself to go in there and start cleaning up. I just needed to get back to the ward and see Leo. I wanted to be there when he woke up and for him to know that he wasn't alone and that I cared about him. I went into his room and threw a few clothes, pyjamas, toiletries and a couple of books into a bag for him and then drove back to the hospital.

When I walked into his cubicle, Alex was sitting there and Leo was still fast asleep.

'He's not woken up at all,' she told me. 'Let's go and grab a quick coffee, Maggie, before I head back to the office.'

We sat in the hospital café and I stared into the polystyrene cup of thick gloopy coffee feeling numb.

'Saying goodbye to Amelie and Lexie was too much for him,' I told her. 'It was too overwhelming. Perhaps we should have sent him to school and not had him there when they said goodbye,' I sighed.

'Well, I think we did the right thing,' replied Alex. 'I'm glad he was with you at home and not at school when he did this. There are far more opportunities at school to get his hands on things that he could use to hurt himself. At least you found him quickly and got him help.'

As Alex talked, I couldn't stop myself from yawning. It was only mid-afternoon but I was shattered.

'Maggie, you must be exhausted after everything that's happened today,' Alex told me, looking concerned. 'This must have all been such a shock for you. Why don't you go home and try to get some sleep?'

'I don't want to leave Leo,' I told her. 'I'm happy to stay with him overnight.'

'The doctor said he's probably going to sleep it off,' she replied. 'You should do that too. Everything will seem better in the morning.'

I knew what she was saying made sense so after I'd sat with Leo for another hour, I headed home. As soon as I walked in the door, my mobile rang. I quickly fished it out of my handbag, worried that it was the hospital trying to get hold of me. But it was my supervising social worker, Becky.

'I've just heard about Leo, Maggie,' she told me. 'Do you want me to pop in for a chat?'

'Do you mind?' I asked her.

'Not at all,' she said.

I knew it would help me to talk it through with someone. Becky arrived fifteen minutes later.

'I feel so guilty,' I told her once I'd made us both a cup of tea. 'I only left him upstairs the amount of time it took me to make a hot chocolate but given the circumstances I shouldn't have left him alone.'

'Maggie, you don't have to justify yourself,' Becky told me. 'It wasn't your fault. He's thirteen years old. You can't be with him 24/7.'

'But I should have known,' I sighed.

'You did your best, Maggie. How could you have known?'

'Because he was so devastated at being separated from his sisters,' I cried, feeling my eyes fill with tears. 'He'd just said goodbye to them and he was absolutely gutted. I knew this was wrong from the start. We should never have split them up.'

'You must stop blaming yourself,' she told me firmly. 'I know you were always worried about how this would impact on Leo, but none of us could have predicted that he would react quite this badly. You've done everything you can for these children, and nobody could have expected any more. I know it's hard, Maggie, but what's done is done.'

By the time Becky left, I felt a little bit better.

After she'd gone, I knew there was something else I needed to do. I took a deep breath and walked into the girls' bedroom. There was so much blood everywhere it looked like a crime scene. There was hot chocolate splattered on the walls and the carpet, while the mattress on the bottom bunk was soaked in Leo's blood. I put on some rubber gloves and pulled the mattress protector off and put it in a bin bag. Then I washed down the walls and sprayed carpet cleaner on the bloodstains to try and get them out.

Afterwards, I was so exhausted I slumped in front of the TV with a sandwich as I was too tired to cook. When my phone beeped, I leapt on it, worried that it was Alex or the hospital trying to get hold of me. I was surprised to see a message from Sally. I felt guilty that in all of the drama, I hadn't had the time or the headspace to think about Amelie and Lexie and how they were getting on in their new home.

Girls have settled brilliantly. They're in bed, fast asleep. Hope all is OK with you and Leo xx

For confidentiality reasons I couldn't tell them anything about Leo and what had happened, and I also didn't want to take away from their excitement and happiness.

Brilliant news, I wrote. *Enjoy xx*

That night I slept for ten hours straight and when I woke up, I felt much better. I went straight to the hospital to see Leo as soon as I was dressed. He still looked very pale but he was awake and talking.

'How are you feeling, lovey?' I asked him gently.

'I'm sorry, Maggie,' he whispered. 'I'm so sorry.'

'You've got nothing to be sorry about,' I told him. 'You gave me a fright, but the main thing is that you're OK.'

Before long, Alex arrived to see him.

'How long do I have to stay in here?' he asked us.

'The doctors have said it's going to be another night until you can come home,' I told him.

Leo shook his head and looked panicked.

'I don't want to go back to that house,' he babbled. 'I want to stay with you, Maggie, but please can we go and live somewhere else? Can you move to a different house and I can come too?'

Alex and I looked at each other.

'Why don't you want to go back to Maggie's, Leo?' Alex asked him gently.

'Cos it makes me feel too sad,' he said, his eyes filling up with tears. 'Everything will remind me of my sisters. I don't think I can stand it.'

I could see even the thought of it was making Leo stressed and he was struggling to breathe.

'Leo, it's OK,' I soothed, stroking his back. 'Take big deep breaths. It's going to be OK.'

I was worried he was going to have a panic attack, but gradually his breathing stabilised.

'Let's take it one day at a time,' Alex told him. 'We know you're going to be here for another night, then we can work out what's going to happen from there.'

Alex and I went outside to have a chat.

'We have to respect what he's saying,' Alex told me. 'We can't force him to go back to your house if he doesn't want to.'

'I can completely understand it,' I sighed. 'Everywhere he looks it will remind him of what he's lost. I'll be so sad not to have him back but our main priority is to keep him safe.

'I'm not a specialist in self-harm,' I told her. 'I can't monitor him through the night.'

Alex looked deep in thought.

'Rather than trying to find him another foster carer, I think we need to be looking at a place in a therapeutic children's home,' she told me.

These were specialist children's homes that were geared up for children with mental health issues. At a specialist home, Leo would have someone with him twenty-four hours a day. There were no locks on the doors and someone would even take him to the toilet to make sure he didn't do anything to hurt himself. There was lots of group work and access to therapists at all times so children could talk about how they were feeling. Homes like this tended to be very small and offered vulnerable children the high level of one-to-one support they needed.

'I'm going to go back to the office now and check if there are any spaces available,' she told me.

I felt desperately sad at the thought of Leo leaving, but at the same time, it was a relief. In all honesty, I didn't think I could keep him safe at my house any more. I would be scared to go to bed at night in case he self-harmed. We couldn't wait any longer for him to connect with his CAMHS therapist. He needed immediate help and he would get that at one of these homes. Perhaps in the long term he could be moved out to a foster carer, but in the short term this was what he needed.

When I was back at home later that afternoon, Alex rang me.

'We got lucky,' she told me. 'Someone is leaving tomorrow so I managed to secure Leo a place at Field Gate House.'

'That's brilliant.' I smiled. 'I think I've heard of that place. Is that the one based on a farm where the children do a lot of their therapy with the animals?'

'Yes, that's it,' replied Alex.

It was a small therapeutic children's home based on a farm in a village about half an hour's drive from me. It provided specialist support for eleven- to sixteen-year-olds and only took six children at a time.

'We need to go up to the hospital and tell Leo,' she told me.

'Do you mind if I take him there tomorrow, if he's happy with that?' I asked.

I didn't want him to feel like I was abandoning him and I wanted to reassure him that I would stay in touch and visit him.

'Absolutely,' said Alex. 'I don't want him to lose his relationship with you.'

It would be another huge change for him and I had no idea how he was going to react to the news.

We met at the hospital half an hour later. Leo was surprised to see us both back again.

'Leo, we need to talk about what's going to happen tomorrow,' Alex told him. 'We know you don't want to go back to Maggie's house as that's where your sisters were. But that's Maggie's home. She owns that house and she can't just move.'

'Please, Maggie,' he begged. 'We can just go and live somewhere else.'

'I can't flower, I'm sorry,' I told him. 'It's my home and where I need to be living. But Alex has found somewhere amazing for you to go.'

She gently told him all about Field Gate House. His ears pricked up when she mentioned it was a farm and that he'd get to look after the animals.

'What sort of animals?' he asked.

'Oh, there are horses and cows, pigs and chickens,' she told him.

'I've heard it's a really calm, lovely place,' I added. 'And there will be lots of staff there who will be able to help keep you safe and do lots of talking with you about how you're feeling.'

Leo nodded.

'Will I see you ever again?' he asked me, tears pricking his eyes.

'Of course you will.' I smiled. 'I'll take you there tomorrow and stay with you for a little while and then I'll come and visit you.'

'Do I have to live there forever?' he asked.

Alex shook her head.

'Let's just get you there first and then in time we can work out a plan. Does that sound OK?'

Leo nodded. It was more change and upheaval for him, but he'd taken the news far better than I'd ever have expected.

EIGHTEEN

Healing

I felt a deep sense of sadness. I still couldn't believe that the girls had gone and now Leo wouldn't be coming back either. I'd known he would be leaving me one day, but it all felt so sudden.

I'd spent all last night packing his things into boxes and they were now all loaded into the boot of the car.

The night before, I'd given Carol a ring.

'I really hope we're doing the right thing for him,' I'd told her.

'It sounds like you didn't have any other option,' she said. 'He'll be OK, Maggie.'

I desperately hoped that she was right. I knew the home would be able to support him with his self-harm and eating issues, and he'd finally get the help he so desperately needed. I just didn't want him to feel rejected or that I was abandoning him.

I picked him up from the hospital and helped him into the car. His arm was still all bandaged up, and he winced as he fastened his seatbelt.

'How far away is it?' he asked nervously.

'Not far, I don't think,' I told him, typing the postcode into the sat nav.

After twenty minutes, we were out of the city and into the open countryside.

'It's so pretty around here,' I sighed as we passed fields full of sheep and cows.

Eventually we drove up a dirt track and I could see there was a large red brick farmhouse at the end of it. There was a path leading up to the front door and a front garden with beds filled with vegetables and rows of brightly coloured flowers.

'What a lovely place,' I exclaimed as we pulled up into the gravel car park.

Leo lingered hesitantly behind me as I started walking up the path.

'Come on.' I smiled. 'Let's go in and say hello.'

We had to press a buzzer and speak into an intercom before the door opened. We walked into a large hallway and a woman came out to meet us. She was dressed casually in shorts, T-shirt and trainers.

'Hi, I'm Annemarie, the manager here.' She smiled. 'You must be Leo.'

He nodded nervously.

'I'm Maggie. What a lovely place.'

'Come with me and I'll give you a tour round,' she told us. 'It's very quiet at the moment as everyone is out on the farm seeing to the animals.'

There was a big kitchen with a huge wooden table in the middle of it. A grey-haired woman was sprinkling cheese on top of what looked like a lasagne.

'We all eat in here together,' Annemarie told us.

'This is Shirley, our cook. She makes the most delicious food and we all take it in turns to help her in the kitchen.'

'Something smells good,' I said.

'This is today's lunch,' replied Shirley. 'Hello, young man,' she said, turning to Leo. 'Would you like a drink or a biscuit? I've just baked some chocolate chip cookies.'

'No thanks,' he said shyly.

Annemarie showed us the other rooms downstairs. There was a big living area with sofas and comfy chairs, a big TV and a huge pile of DVDs.

'This is where everyone hangs out,' she told Leo.

There were a couple of other smaller rooms that I guessed were used for therapy sessions, as well as a large office for the staff. It all seemed very cosy and calm. There were plants everywhere and vases of flowers and lots of art on the walls that looked like it might have been done by some of the children who had lived there.

There was also a large room with a big bank of desks in it.

'This is our classroom, where a tutor comes in every day and works with you,' she told us.

'So I won't have to go to my school any more?' he asked.

'No, sweetie, for now you're going to do everything here,' I told him.

Annemarie took us upstairs to look at the bedrooms.

'This is going to be your room, Leo,' she told him.

It was large room with two single beds in it, a huge wardrobe, two chests of drawers and a double desk running along the window.

'You'll be sharing it with a boy called James,' she said. 'He's twelve.'

I walked over to the window.

'You've got a lovely view overlooking the fields,' I told him.

'Right, I'll leave you to unpack and when you feel ready, Leo, you can come down,' she told us. 'It will be lunchtime in an hour so you can meet everybody then.'

Leo looked a bit overwhelmed.

'What do you think?' I asked him, once Annemarie had left.

'It seems nice,' he said, sounding uncertain.

'Don't worry, give it time and you'll settle in.'

While he explored his bedroom, I fetched some of his stuff in from the car.

'Oh, you brought my bear,' he said as he pulled it out of one of the boxes.

'Of course I did,' I told him. 'Your sisters would be cross if you didn't bring him with you.'

He pressed the bear's tummy.

'We love you, Leo!' boomed the familiar voices and suddenly he looked sad.

'Do you think Amelie and Lexie are OK?' he asked forlornly.

'I think they're absolutely fine,' I told him. 'I'm sure they're missing you like you're missing them, but I'm sure Simon and Sally will be taking good care of them.'

Leo looked deep in thought.

'Can I phone them, Maggie, and tell them I'm not at your house any more?' he asked.

'You can write to them and I'll pass it on to Alex to give to them,' I told him. 'And maybe in time they can come and visit you here. Would you like that?'

Leo looked shocked. 'What, Amelie and Lexie could come here?' he gasped.

'There are no guarantees, but I could certainly ask if that would be possible,' I told him. 'Do you think they'd like it?'

'Oh, they'd love it.' He smiled. 'They'd love the animals and running round the fields.'

He frowned. 'You won't tell them though, will you?' he asked, pointing to his bandaged arm with an ashamed look on his face. 'I don't want them to know what I did to myself. You won't tell them will you, Maggie? I don't want them to be sad and worried.'

'No one will tell them Leo,' I reassured him. 'They don't need to know.'

That seemed to reassure him.

I stayed with him for another hour to check that he was OK. We couldn't unpack his things as Annemarie had said she needed to go through his stuff with him and check there was nothing in there that he could use to hurt himself with.

'But you packed my things, Maggie,' Leo frowned, looking confused.

'I know, lovey, but they just need to double-check,' I told him. 'Remember you're here so they can help you and keep you safe and that's what they have to do with everyone who comes to live here.'

After an hour, it was time for me to go.

'Do you have to?' he asked, looking panicked.

'You'll be having lunch soon and Annemarie's going to introduce you to everyone.' I smiled. 'You don't want me getting in the way.'

He looked tired, bewildered and lost.

'Will I ever see you again, Maggie?' he asked.

'Of course you will, silly,' I said. 'I'll be back in a couple of days to visit you. You're not going to get rid of me that easily.'

He gave me a weak smile and I wrapped my arms around him.

'You're going to be absolutely fine, lovey,' I told him. 'This is a fresh start.'

As I got into the car, I looked up at the bedroom window where Leo was watching. I waved and blew him a kiss.

'See you soon, Leo,' I shouted.

I did my best to put a smile on my face, but as I drove back down the winding country line, I didn't have to keep up the pretence any longer. I pulled into a layby and let the tears stream down my face.

I was crying for Leo, and for Lexie and Amelie, and for everything that had happened. At times, the last few days had felt like a nightmare. Had we done the right thing for the children?

I couldn't bear the thought of going back to an empty house so I called in at Carol's.

'Oh, Maggie, love,' she sighed when she opened the door and saw my red puffy face.

'I feel so awful leaving him there on his own,' I sobbed.

It wasn't the way I'd intended to say goodbye to Leo. Things had ended so suddenly.

'He's in the best place,' she soothed, hugging me tightly. 'They can give him the specialist help that he needs.'

I knew she was right, but it didn't stop me missing him or worrying about him. He'd been through so much and he was so vulnerable – I wanted the best for him.

I felt exhausted and still horribly guilty that I had been part of causing all his pain. Had it been worth it? Yes, Amelie and Lexie had a new life with Sally and Simon, but at what cost to Leo?

There and then I vowed that I would never knowingly be part of a split adoption again. Going forward, I was determined that I would fight tooth and nail to keep sibling groups together. I knew I could never go through this process again. Looking after Leo, Lexie and Amelie had profoundly affected me and changed how I felt about adoption. It had been one of the most painful things that I'd ever had to do in my fostering career, and I knew I couldn't be part of causing that much anguish and upset to a child ever again.

Epilogue

There was a crunch of gravel as a car pulled up into the driveway.

'They're here!' yelled Leo, who had been keeping watch at the window for the past half an hour.

He ran out of the room and bolted down the stairs and I quickly followed him. Simon and Sally got out of the front and as they opened the back doors, Lexie and Amelie jumped out along with a very excitable black collie.

'Leo!' the girls yelled as they both ran over to him smiling.

'This is Trixie,' Lexie told him and they all bent down and made a fuss of the dog.

I walked over to Simon and Sally and smiled.

'What a lovely place,' said Sally, looking around.

'It really is. I'm so thankful that they had space for Leo.'

'How's he doing?' asked Simon. 'We were so sorry to hear about what happened.'

Alex had filled them in.

'It's been hard for him, but he's doing OK.' I shrugged. 'It's going to take a long time but he's on the right path.'

It had been a couple of months since the girls and Leo had left my house. He'd struggled to settle in at first, mainly due to the constant monitoring and endless therapy. But I'd visited him every week and he got on well with his roommate James. As the days went by, he started to look healthier and was slowly putting on weight.

I watched as the three of them ran round with Trixie, laughing.

'Thank you for bringing the girls,' I said to them. 'I think seeing them will really help him.'

'We wanted to,' replied Sally. 'I know how much they miss him.'

'We've had lots of wobbles and ups and downs with them,' agreed Simon. 'I think once the novelty wore off, it finally hit them what they'd been through and what they'd lost. We're working through it and generally they seem happy.'

'Good.' I smiled. 'I'm glad.'

'There's still a sadness there about them not being with their brother and I think perhaps there always will be,' sighed Sally.

I could see the three of them were delighted to be back together again. Leo was excited to show them around the farm and tell them all about the animals he was working with. He even took us into the kitchen and showed us the big plate of scones that he'd helped Shirley to make.

'Try one,' he said.

He got some jam out of the fridge and gave the girls one each. I watched with delight as he tucked into one too.

Since he'd come to the home, his eating was gradually improving. As part of his treatment, they'd got him involved in picking the food and cooking it and that had really seemed to help.

'Do you live here now, Leo?' asked Amelie, amazed.

'Yes,' he said.

'Wow, you're so lucky,' she told him.

I couldn't help but notice the angry red scar on the underside of his arm as he spoke animatedly with his sisters.

His stitches had been taken out a few weeks after the incident, but a couple of months on, the scar was still red and swollen. It would always be there, a permanent reminder to him of what had happened and what he'd lost. But scars fade, and in time it would slowly turn from angry red to white. In the same way, I hoped Leo's pain and hurt would heal as the months and years passed. He would never, ever forget his sisters; he would always be their protector and big brother, but seeing them running out happily into the fields together, I hoped that now he'd finally be able to find a way to move on without them.

Acknowledgements

Thank you to my children, Tess, Pete and Sam, who are such a big part of my fostering today. However, I had not met you when Leo, Amelie, Lexie and Louisa came into my home. Thanks to my wide circle of fostering friends – you know who you are! Your support and your laughter are valued. Thanks to my friend Andrew B for your continued encouragement and care. Thanks also to Heather Bishop, who spent many hours listening and enabled this story to be told, my literary agent Rowan Lawton, and to Anna Valentine and Marleigh Price at Trapeze for giving me the opportunity to share these stories.

A Note from Maggie

I really hope you enjoyed reading Leo, Lexie and Amelie's story. I love sharing my experiences of fostering with you, and I also love hearing what you think about them. If you enjoyed this book, or any of my others, please think about leaving a review online. I know other readers really benefit from your thoughts, and I do too.

To be the first to hear about my new books, you can keep in touch on my Facebook page @MaggieHartleyAuthor. I find it inspiring to learn about your own experiences of fostering and adoption, and to read your comments and reviews.

Finally, thank you so much for choosing to read *Please Don't Take My Sisters*. If you enjoyed it, there are others available including *Too Scared to Cry, Tiny Prisoners, The Little Ghost Girl, A Family for Christmas, Too Young to be a Mum, Who Will Love Me Now, The Girl No One Wanted, Battered, Broken, Healed, Is It My Fault Mummy?, Sold to be a Wife, Denied a Mummy* and *Daddy's Little Soldier*. I hope you'll enjoy my next story just as much.

Maggie Hartley